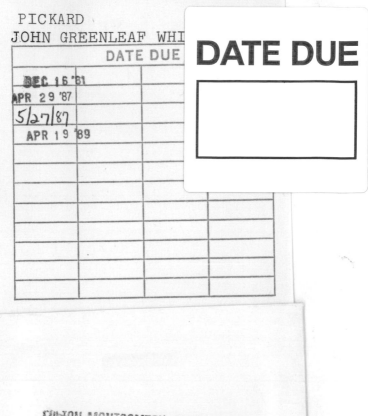

AMERICAN AUTHORS AND CRITICS SERIES

Published by Barnes & Noble under the general editorship of FOSTER PROVOST *and* JOHN MAHONEY *of Duquesne University with the sponsorship of that university*

ABOUT THE AUTHOR

JOHN B. PICKARD is Assistant Professor of English at Rice University and the author of several articles published in professional journals. He is the grandson of Samuel T. Pickard, Whittier's official biographer, and Elizabeth Whittier Pickard, Whittier's niece.

John Greenleaf Whittier in 1856

JOHN GREENLEAF WHITTIER

An Introduction and Interpretation

JOHN B. PICKARD

Barnes & Noble, Inc.   New York

Publishers   Booksellers   Since 1873

PREFACE

Appreciation is expressed to Harry Hayden Clark for his critical suggestions and constant encouragement, and to Miss Patricia Harris of Barnes & Noble and Drs. Foster Provost and John Mahoney for their editorial and critical assistance throughout all stages of the book.

Sections of this book have previously appeared as articles and acknowledgment is made to the following journals for permission to reprint these articles in somewhat revised form: "Whittier's Ballads: The Maturing of an Artist," *Essex Institute Historical Collections* (January, 1960); "Imagistic and Structural Unity in 'Snow-Bound,'" *College English* (March, 1960); "Whittier's Critical Creed: The Beauty of the Commonplace and the Truth of Style," *Rice Institute Pamphlet* (October, 1960).

Grateful acknowledgment is made to Houghton Mifflin Company for permission to use the portrait of Whittier which faces page 122 and the photograph of his Amesbury home. Appreciation is also given to the Trustees of the John Greenleaf Whittier Homestead for permission to use the interior view of Whittier's birthplace.

Whittier's birthplace near Haverhill and his home at Amesbury are owned by the Trustees of the John Greenleaf Whittier Homestead and the Whittier Home Association, respectively, and may be visited by the public.

J. B. P.

CONTENTS

ILLUSTRATIONS

CHRONOLOGY

1807 John Greenleaf Whittier born December 17, on a farm near Haverhill, Massachusetts, the second child of poor Quaker parents. The Whittiers had been in New England since 1638.

1814–15 Entered district school for a few winter months of education.

1821 Introduced to Burns's poetry which stimulated first verse writings.

1826 In June published his first poem, "The Exile's Departure," in William Lloyd Garrison's *Newburyport Free Press*. Beginning of friendship between Garrison and Whittier.

1826–27 Published over eighty poems in local papers, most of them imitations of Scott, Byron, and the American Romantics.

1827–28 Enrolled at Haverhill Academy. Supported self for two terms by schoolteaching and shoemaking. Friendships and unfulfilled romances with Mary Emerson Smith and Evelina Bray.

1829 Edited *The American Manufacturer* in Boston. Continued writing poetry.

1830 Edited the *Haverhill Gazette* for six months. Father died. Appointed editor of influential *New England Review* in Hartford. Greatly widened his social, political, and literary acquaintances under the influence of Mrs. Sigourney. Actively supported Clay for president over Jackson.

1831 Published his first book, *Legends of New England,* and chosen as a delegate to National Republican Convention.

1832 Resigned editorship in ill health. Unsuccessful attempt to win a congressional seat in place of Caleb Cushing.

1833 Joined the Anti-Slavery party upon Garrison's urging. Published *Justice and Expediency* in June, wrote first Abolitionist verses, and served as a delegate to the first meeting of the American Anti-Slavery Convention in December.

1835 Served as member of the Massachusetts legislature. In September, mobbed and stoned with George Thompson in Concord, New Hampshire.

1836   Sold farm and moved to Amesbury, which remained his home until death.

1837   Worked in New York and Philadelphia for the Abolitionists and met Elizabeth Lloyd and Lucy Hooper.

1838   First authorized collection of his poetry, *Poems*, published. Became editor of the *Pennsylvania Freeman*. Office burned and sacked in May.

1839   Broke with Garrison over use of political power and helped form the Liberty party as a political-action group of the Abolitionist party.

1840   Resigned editorship in ill health and returned to Amesbury. This ended his most active participation in the Abolitionist movement.

1843   Helped to defeat Caleb Cushing's nomination as Secretary of the Treasury. Published *Lays of My Home* and renewed his interest in genre subjects and local ballads.

1844–45   Editor of the *Middlesex Standard* in Lowell.

1846   Published *Voices of Freedom*.

1847   Joined the *National Era* as corresponding editor. Published most of his prose and poetry in this paper for the next ten years.

1849   Finished main prose writing with the publication of *Margaret Smith's Journal*.

1850   Published *Songs of Labor*. During the 1850's Whittier emerged as the poet of the commonplace, writing some of his best verses —"Maud Muller," "Telling the Bees," "Skipper Ireson's Ride," "The Last Walk in Autumn," and "The Double-Headed Snake of Newbury." Persuaded Charles Sumner to run for senate and Sumner was elected in 1851.

1857   Assured of a wide reading public with founding of the *Atlantic Monthly*. Mother died.

1858–59   Renewed friendship with Elizabeth Lloyd and seriously considered marriage.

1860   Published *Home Ballads*, a collection of his poetry from the 1850's.

1863   "Barbara Frietchie" published.

1864   Sister Elizabeth died.

1866   Gained financial security with the great popular success of *Snow-Bound*.

1867 Achieved best-seller status with *The Tent on the Beach.*

1868 Published *Among the Hills.* Increasing interest in devotional writing.

1872 Published *The Pennsylvania Pilgrim, and Other Poems,* which contained "The Brewing of Soma."

1876 Began spending winter months at Oak Knoll in Danvers. Published *Mabel Martin.*

1881 Published *The King's Missive, and Other Poems.*

1886 Honorary LL.D. from Harvard.

1888–89 Issued definitive edition of his prose and poetry in seven volumes.

1890 Privately printed his last book, *At Sundown.*

1892 Very ill during the winter. Suffered a stroke in September and died on September 7, at Hampton Falls, New Hampshire. Buried in the family plot at Amesbury.

And now, with autumn's moonlit eves,
  Its harvest-time has come,
We pluck away the frosted leaves,
  And bear the treasure home.
              —*The Corn-Song,* THE HUSKERS

✍ INTRODUCTION

F OR MOST Americans John Greenleaf Whittier is associated with grammar school memories of stuffy, overcrowded rooms with their jumble of slate blackboards, maps, and squirming children. If pushed further some might recall a steel-etched engraving of a stern, elderly man dressed in an old-fashioned broadcloth coat, whose piercing eyes dominated a full white beard. The most retentive might dredge up some curious singsong snatches of "Blessings on thee, little man," or " 'Shoot, if you must, this old gray head,/But spare your country's flag,' she said," once dutifully memorized and fervently recited. Now such memories would probably elicit an amused smile and careless dismissal. Yet for many modern critics these associations typify the oppressive, even malign, effect that constant exposure to mediocre poetry has had on popular poetic taste. Perhaps Whittier and the other New England poets have been justly discredited for their sentimentality, pietism, diffuse rhetoric, and stock characterizations. Certainly artistic and historical perspective has correctly measured them against the masters of nineteenth-century verse, Poe, Whitman, and Dickinson, and found them to be minor rather than major figures.

Ironically, Whittier completely agreed with the current low estimate of his artistic merits. He considered "Maud Muller" not worth serious analysis, wondered if the famed simplicity of "Telling the Bees" weren't silliness instead, and doubted if "In School-Days" fitted his solemn Quaker personality. An overall view of his achievement which Whittier once gave a friend might well have been written directly for his modern detractors:

> We shall perish, and verily *our words will follow us*. The hearts which now know us and love us will also soon cease to beat, and with them our very memories will die. The utilitarian of the twentieth century will not heed whether, in treading on our graves, he shakes the dust of prose or poetry from his feet. And after all what matters it? Who cares for the opinion of the twentieth century? Not I, for one.

Constantly Whittier insisted that he was a man, not a mere verse-maker, that he placed a "higher value on my name as appended to the Anti-Slavery Declaration . . . than on the title-page of any book." Humanitarian and reformer he definitely was and his most recent biographers have chosen to accentuate these facets of his personality. Their emphasis on the trenchant Abolitionist editor, the practical politician, the fiery agitator for liberal reform, and the fervid defender of democratic liberties has all but obscured the poet. The harvest of new information in these biographies has fully portrayed Whittier as a part of his age and reconciled the old paradoxes of how the passive Quaker could be the militant fighter and how the reserved "wood-thrush of Essex" could begin as the melancholic Byronic versifier, only to side-step a more perplexing problem: are there valid literary reasons for continuing to examine Whittier's best poems on a mature level beyond his historical and cultural interest?

Posing this question of artistic merit by no means allows an easy answer. However, if one honestly weighs standards of taste in the nineteenth century, fully admits Whittier's glaring flaws, and then assesses his poetry in the light of modern critical techniques, a surprising number of Whittier's poems do justify continued study. A sympathetic critic once remarked that Whittier was "one-third American democrat, one-third sheer dullness, and one-third genuine poet." It is the hope of this book to resurrect that last important fraction.

2

1

≪§ FORMATIVE YEARS

M ORE THAN any other writer of the nineteenth century Whittier was essentially a product of his age, a fact which makes a broad historical setting necessary to a proper view of him. Born in 1807, he grew up in a period of intense nationalism and sectional self-confidence. During the era of "good feeling" which followed the War of 1812, the growing power of the common man culminated in the election of Andrew Jackson as President and the founding of a truly democratic party. This period saw the opening of the Erie Canal, the beginnings of the great expansion to the West, the rapid development of heavy industry, and the first surge of large-scale immigration. Under the impact of material growth and the increasing power of the new middle class, the harsh doctrines of Calvinism were replaced by a softer, more acceptable humanitarianism. Now religion stressed man, not God; heaven, not hell; and brotherhood and social responsibility were the important commandments. The pietism and sentimentality engendered by these new religious movements found expression in numerous reform groups which agitated for everything from abolishment of slavery and cockfighting to the establishment of woman suffrage and utopian communities.

Literature, as well as religion and politics, reflected the nationalistic demands for an American culture divorced from European influences. In 1828 an immature Whittier echoed this desire by trumpeting America's potential for a native literature:

> It has often been said that the New World is deficient in poetry and romance; that its bards must of necessity linger over the classic ruins of other lands; and draw their sketches of character from foreign sources, and paint Nature under the soft beauty of an Eastern sky. On the contrary New England is full of Romance. . . . we have mountains pillaring a sky as blue as that which bends over classic Olympus; streams as bright and beautiful as those of Greece or Italy—and forests richer and nobler than those which of old were haunted by Sylph and Dryad.

Notwithstanding, the vogue for English authors increased. The colorful dramatic tales of Sir Walter Scott stirred the idealistic, adventurous nature of the American people; the narrative power and defiant egotism of Byron's poetry thrilled and shocked them; and the sentimental graveyard poetry of Mrs. Hemans caused them to weep. In the wake of the English Romantics followed a host of American imitators, Whittier among them.

Moreover, the critical and philosophical ideas of the leading English Romantics gave American writers a theoretical basis for their literary approach. Since man was considered the dominant power in the universe, his relationship with the forces of nature was closely studied. Nature furnished the poet with innumerable analogues to man's life, for the smallest leaf displayed the presence of the Divine. The swing to emotionalism, a return to nature, and an emphasis on the individual swept aside the Neoclassic doctrines of restraint and reason. Still, these exciting new ideas were severely curtailed by American popular taste which viewed literature as a safeguard for Christian morality. Pietism and sentimentality were the trade-marks of any book, as they were the props supporting the religious interests of the people. Since the fiction of the time was meant to inspire, to stress homely virtues, and to invent "decent" romantic fantasies, critics and reviewers echoed these sentiments by insisting that literature conform to prevailing religious standards and by censuring authors for any deviations. Readers were darkly warned about the licentious lives of Byron and Shelley and the amoral quality of their works. The best literature was of a practical and social nature, inspired by Christian principle and reflecting its optimism and hope. Simple ideas and ease in reading were demanded by popular taste. James Russell Lowell was only echoing the American public when he stated, "The proof of poetry is, in my mind, that it reduce to the essence of a single line the vague philosophy which is floating in all men's minds, and so render it portable and ready to the hand." Such were the critical sentiments and popular attitudes of the age in which Whittier reached maturity.

≈§ §≈

   The farmhouse in which Whittier was born, near Haverhill, Massachusetts, was typical of the thousands of similar homesteads scattered throughout rural New England. Solidly erected of hand-hewn logs, it was already nearly one hundred and twenty years old. The farm itself was set in a natural valley, almost surrounded by hills, with the nearest neighbor a half-mile distant. This enforced isolation bound the Whittiers to one spot, making them fully dependent on one another for companionship, entertainment, and even education. Strong, intangible links with the past also united the Whittiers. The family had come to New England in 1638 and since then had been continuously associated with the Merrimack River Valley section of northeast Massachusetts. Through the years the characteristics of the region had become the Whittiers': a tenacious spirit of independence that demanded and obtained local government; a hard-won awareness of the value of rigorous work and simple living; a flintlike determination to secure the natural rights of man; and a practical knowledge of human nature that closeness to elemental forces brings.

   Intimately connected with this New England heritage, and even more important for his future development, was Whittier's Quaker background. In the Puritan theocracy of seventeenth-century New England the Quaker settler had been a nonconformist. Denying the Calvinistic insistence on the innate depravity of man and a wrathful Old Testament God, he had even subordinated the Bible to the Inner Light and had rejected the tenet that priestly rule is necessary for salvation. For these heretical views the early Quakers suffered exile, personal humiliation, whipping, mutilation, and even hanging. These excesses occasioned a wave of sympathy for the passive victims which was aided by the relaxation of church control over government and the increasing secularization of society. By the eighteenth century, trade and finance, rather than

Whittier's Birthplace, Scene of "Snow-Bound," Haverhill, Massachusetts

salvation and theology, were man's chief interests; and the Quaker concept of a personal God and the brotherhood of man won many converts. The first Whittier in New England, though not a Quaker, was deprived of his voting rights in 1652 for his uncompromising disapproval of the persecutions of the Quakers. Eventually his sympathy, coupled with the later marriage of a son, Joseph Whittier, to a Quakeress, led future Whittier generations into the Society of Friends. Whittier's parents were devout Quakers who held daily worship at home and who attended First Day meetings in Amesbury regardless of weather or the discomfort of a nine-mile journey. Also Whittier read and literally made a part of his being the six Quaker books in his father's small library. The writings of Penn, Baxter, Chalkley, and others schooled Whittier in the essence of Quakerism: the necessity of individual striving for self-perfection rather than a blind adherence to outward rules and formalized creeds; the importance of the New Testament Christ of love and compassion; the humanitarian practice of social equality and freedom of speech and religion; the emphasis on simplicity of dress and manners to indicate an inner spiritual humility; and the necessity of viewing all aspects of life from a spiritual plane. These basic ideas directly influenced Whittier's life by causing his early enlistment in the Abolitionist movement and by occasioning some of the finest religious lyrics of his mature years. Also the knowledge of Quaker history furnished him with backgrounds and narratives for many of his best ballads. Even Whittier's concept of literature and style was affected by these journals, for their authors taught him to appreciate books which were "shorn of all ornament, simple and direct as the contrition and prayer of childhood." Whittier fully absorbed the basic literary philosophy permeating the Quaker journals as explained by William Penn in his preface to *The Written Gospel Labours of John Whitehead*. Penn believed that the Quakers should avoid a display of learning, exclude from their pages all ornaments of style and diction, and convey to the reader the feeling of inner peace and quiet which Quakerism teaches. Literature should inspire devotion and explore the beauty of holiness and truth. Such was the lasting harvest which Whittier gathered from these few books and his taciturn father might well have unbended to compliment his son's thrifty management of such meager literary heritage.

Whittier's farm experiences also formed the man. Though never poverty-stricken, Whittier's father was unable to free his farm from debt and only the strictest economy and husbandry kept the farm alive. Under such conditions Whittier's youth was hardly the equivalent of the idyllic barefoot boyhood portrayed in his rustic poetry. Like all farm boys Whittier had to assume the man-sized burdens of planting, harvesting, and milking. These tasks overstrained his indifferent physical strength and, when he was seventeen, he permanently impaired his health. Unfit for heavy farm labor and increasingly aware that he was temperamentally unsuited to the life of a farmer, it is no wonder that his earliest verses complained:

> And must I always swing the flail,
> And help to fill the milking pail?
> I wish to go away to school;
> I do not wish to be a fool.

But despite his chaffing at the restrictions of farm life and the parochialism of his environment, Whittier reaped innumerable benefits from his farm years. His father's grim determination to master an unyielding soil and his pride in Jeffersonian democracy became the traits of the son. The frugal simplicity which necessity forced upon the young Whittier was a valuable attribute in the mature poet, for until 1865 he was never to earn over five hundred dollars a year. Relaxation from farm chores centered around the evening talk of the family and walks along the Merrimack River. The tales told by his parents and visitors of trips to Canada, Indian raids, haunted bridges, and Quaker persecutions were forever etched upon his impressionable mind. Also his uncle, "innocent of books," supplemented Whittier's few months of formal education with his own understanding and appreciation of nature. He carefully nurtured in the young boy his own love for "the little world of sights and sounds" of the Haverhill district and this affection Whittier never lost. Instinctively Whittier was attracted to the beauty hidden beneath the apparent austerity of his family's life and the plain landscape around him. Yet, sensing the beauty in the old legends, the rural landscape, and the simple Quaker life and acting upon the possibility of transmuting this raw material into moving poetry were two different things. A realization of its inherent poetic value was only to come with his introduction to the poetry of Robert Burns.

This occurred in 1821 when a wandering "pawky auld carle" of a Scotsman sang some of Burns's songs in return for bread and cider. Later in the same year, a local schoolmaster, Joshua Coffin, visited the Whittiers and read some of Burns's poetry from a volume he had with him. The effect upon the boy was instantaneous and as Whittier himself later recalled: "This was about the first poetry I had ever [heard],—with the exception of the Bible, of which I was a close student,—and it had a lasting influence on me. I began to make rhymes myself, and to imagine stories and adventures. In fact I lived a sort of dual life, and in a world of fancy, as well as in the world of plain matter-of-fact about me." This dual life which he started to lead was to vex him throughout his literary career. Always the press of current interests, whether farm tasks, Abolitionist work, editorships, or economic duress, was to militate against his longing to write poetry. Primarily this introduction to Burns initiated the fourteen-year-old farm boy's rhyme-making and dreams of literary fame. At night time when freed from his farm labors, Whittier covered his slate with verses instead of schoolwork. One of his earliest known attempts was a rhymed catalogue of the books he had read. Prophetically the religious section was the longest and opened with:

> The Bible towering o'er the rest,
> Of all the other books the best.

These comments proved truer than the boy could know, for throughout his life the Bible remained the major inspiration for his thought and moral practice, as well as a prime source for his imagery and allusions. Most often the "rhymes" Whittier made were doggerel or direct newspaper imitations, while the range of topics chosen indicates the uncertainty of his taste. Praise for William Penn and early Quaker martyrs was mingled with admiration for Byron and Lafayette. Romantic glimpses of distant lands were contrasted with nationalistic boasting about New England's Nahant beach. By 1826 Whittier had written down nearly thirty of these poems and a year later he had published seventy-six poems. Among these were many attempts to vitalize local legends and superstitions in Burns's manner, including such imitations of it as "The Veil":

9

> Odds leddy! then ye've lost your veil;
> But dinna let your spirits fail;
> What though the auld thing onward sail
>   A mile or twa,
> Your greetin' winna now awail,—
>   Sae let it gae.

These few lines indicate how heavily Whittier was drawing upon Burns: the Scottish dialect, the stanzaic form, and the light humorous subject matter recall Burns's "To a Louse." Similarly many of Whittier's love songs reflect the somewhat sentimental lyrics of Burns. Though most of these early poems are mere rhyming exercises, they illustrate Whittier's attempt to write about his own commonplace experiences and rural section as Burns had sung about his. In Burns Whittier found one of his own kind: a farm boy like himself, with little education, who had ruined his health on a farm and who hated intolerance and hypocrisy. How easy it must have been for Whittier to see under Burns's guidance "the worth/Of life among the lowly," and above all else to perceive "through all familiar things/The romance underlying."

Indeed, the themes, subject matter, and style of Burns had a direct and lasting influence upon Whittier. Burns was a poet who appealed to ordinary people; he wrote of their common thoughts and feelings—dislike of harsh Calvinistic church rule, belief in the innate dignity of man and social equality, disdain for ostentation, and love of nature. His poems, "Halloween," "The Holy Fair," and "Tam O'Shanter," are steeped in local lore, customs, and superstitions; "The Cotter's Saturday Night" dwells tenderly on the simplicity and humility of family virtue. All these themes were to be Whittier's too, but Burns first indicated to Whittier the poetic value of these local tales and folk legends. Though lacking proper style and manner of presentation, Whittier's first book, *Legends of New England* (1831), was based entirely on native material. Moreover, all of Burns's better poems have an underlying realism achieved by the use of the Scottish dialect with its vigorous, richly suggestive native terms, by the manipulation of simple ordinary words, and by the presentation of ideas through visual concrete detail. Also he draws heavily on the familiar objects of the farm and nature as source material for his poetry. His imagery is rarely complex or expansive, though connotative and moving in its simple comparisons. It was these characteristics that were finally to be Whittier's when he had achieved a "truth of style." Unfortunately, however, he was not to follow the path marked by Burns's poetry nor even understand its importance until years later.

Whittier's earliest writings had been encouraged by his older sister Mary who claimed they were as good as those which she read in the weekly newspapers. However, Whittier had done nothing with these pieces beyond putting them in manuscript form and reading them to his family. Finally Mary launched the hesitant author by appropriating one of the best poems, "The Exile's Departure," and sending it in June, 1826, to the *Newburyport Free Press*. The editor of *The Press* was another unknown young man, just publishing his first paper and beginning his long and turbulent career as a humanitarian and reformer—William Lloyd Garrison. The poem was printed in the June 8 issue and Garrison asked for more. An astounded Whittier found himself in print and delightedly sent another poem, "The Deity." Garrison printed this with the comment: "His poetry bears the stamp of true poetic genius, which, if carefully cultivated, will rank him among the bards of his country." Garrison was so impressed with his discovery that he rode out to the Whittier farm, surprising the poet who was on his hands and knees searching for eggs under the barn. Garrison's social tact smoothed an awkward situation as he pleaded with Whittier's parents to encourage the boy's ability and to allow him further education. Penniless and proud, the father could only respond to Garrison's heated argument with the dry observation that poetry would not buy bread. However, as the year went on more of Whittier's poems were published in the *Haverhill Gazette* and the persuasive urgings of its editor were added to those of Garrison. Reluctantly, Whittier's father consented and in 1827 Whittier was allowed to earn his own way through the first term of the newly opened Haverhill Academy.

2

⮴ SOCIAL AND
PROFESSIONAL GROWTH

THE SIX years following Whittier's first term at Haverhill Academy, 1827–33, were the most stimulating, broadening, and restless of his life. He crammed a classical high school education into two short terms. As editor of three New England newspapers, one an outstanding weekly, he entered fully into the social life of Haverhill and Hartford. His astounding output of nearly two hundred poems in addition to editing several books won him wide acclaim. By 1831 Whittier had decided on politics as the quickest route to fame, only to be defeated in his attempts for a Congressional seat. A year later, broken in health, mentally and emotionally exhausted, Whittier, at twenty-five, returned to the farm from which he had so hopefully departed. Abolition was to become his next pursuit.

⮴ ⮳

Whittier's rise from an unpolished, uneducated New England farm boy to a nationally known poet, a highly regarded editor, and a leading candidate for Congress was a startling transformation. The wonder of the change is that Whittier's sensitive and ambition-filled spirit remained stable and modest. Certainly he did bask in the glamour of new-found social opportunity, responding to the romantic attentions of young women in Haverhill, and he was driven by an intense desire for renown which silenced the quiet promptings of his Quaker Inner Light. A portrait of Whittier at twenty-two reveals a finely featured, almost haughty face, marked by an unusually high forehead and thin, sensitive lips and dominated by piercing direct eyes. The effect is one of youthful intensity and unshakable determination. One of his female friends remarked of Whittier at this time:

> He was a very handsome, distinguished-looking young man. His eyes were remarkably beautiful. He was tall, slight, and very erect; a bashful youth, but never awkward. . . . In society he was embarrassed, and his manners were, in consequence, sometimes brusque and cold. With intimate friends he talked a great deal, and in a wonderfully interesting manner; usually earnest, often analytical, and frequently playful. . . . He was very modest, never conceited, never egotistic. One could never flatter him.

Undoubtedly his two years in Haverhill greatly broadened his intellectual range, allowing him to measure his poetic ambitions against the established masters of English literature. Having been publicly praised as a "genius of a high order" in a prospectus for his poems, he must have envisioned poetic fame within his grasp. At the same time he earned his tuition by shoemaking and schoolteaching, frugally calculating his first term expenses to within twenty-five cents. His ready acceptance by the best families and the female response to his sensitivity and refinement gave his shy personality the confidence it badly needed. Still the substance of his dreams must have seemed like tinsel when he realized that his worshipful interest in a distant cousin, Mary Emerson Smith, could result only in friendship. He had known her since childhood and had even once lived at her house while attending district school. As a classmate at the academy, she shepherded him through his awkward social development and in Whittier's own words saw "beneath the clownish exterior something which gave promise of intellect and worth. The powers of my own mind, the mysteries of my own spirit, were revealed to myself, only as they were called out by one of those dangerous relations called cousins, who, with all her boarding school glories upon her, condescended to smile upon my rustic simplicity." However, she was of a superior social class and not a Quaker. Even more chafing must have been the unfulfilled climax to his romance with Evelina Bray, another academy classmate, which foundered again on the hard rocks of his poverty and Quakerism. It is no wonder that Whittier could rhetorically dramatize his position:

> I will *quit poetry, and everything else of a literary manner,* for I am sick at heart of the business. Insult has maddened me. The friendless boy has been mocked at; and years ago he vowed to triumph over the scorners of his boyish endeavors. With the unescapable sense of wrong burning like a volcano in the recesses of his spirit, he has striven to accomplish this vow, until his heart has grown weary of the struggle.

With the completion of his second school term, the failure of the proposed edition of his poetry, and romantic disappointments, Whittier could indeed wonder where he was to go from there. His precarious day-to-day existence was so upset by his awareness of shirking family responsibilities that there was no hope for a college education. Fortunately Garrison again came to his rescue and secured for Whittier the editorship of a Boston weekly, *The American Manufacturer,* in 1829. Somewhat incongruously, Whittier was cast as an advocate for Clay's plan for a high tariff to protect growing American industry against the popular democracy of Andrew Jackson. The editorship was a complete education, since Whittier had to be his own typesetter, proofreader, book reviewer, news analyst, poetry writer, and office boy. Though much of the paper was devoted to routine accounts of business transactions and careful "scissors" selection from other newspapers, Whittier's articles reveal his deepening political and economic thinking, growing interest in reform, and increasing awareness of national affairs. Of the American system Whittier could write:

> If there is any situation truly enviable, it is that of the industrious mechanic, who by his own, unaided exertions, has established for himself a respectable place in society, who, commencing in poverty, has been able by his own skill and perseverance to overcome every obstacle, to vanquish every prejudice. . . . Industry and virtuous ambition are seldom exerted in vain.

A series of similar naive and optimistic articles were addressed to these young mechanics. At the same time his lyrics romanticized poetic fancy and darkly pondered death and churchyard burials.

14

Yet declaiming in the journalistic manner, Whittier castigated the "want of strength and boldness in our poetical writers." This article on "American Literature" hit directly at the reasons for this failure, and unconsciously at his own major flaws, when it commented on the "dangerous encouragement which is given to the light flashes of fancy—the tinsel and drapery of poetry, without the substance." Although he was editor for just seven months, he not only served his apprenticeship but made this relatively obscure weekly paper widely admired for its selection of news and leading articles. Though he was living in Boston his Quaker shyness and the pressures of his job curtailed his social life and restrained his poetic daydreaming. Still the attractions of a sophisticated, worldly-wise manner remained, for he could rhapsodize on the "airy motions" and dark beauty of Boston women and remark: "I have become a notable fellow in gallantry of late . . . I have given my whiskers a more ferocious appearance."

During the next year, spent at home, Whittier became the editor of the *Essex Gazette*. He continued his espousal of humanitarian reform and widened his literary interests with articles on Cooper, Shelley, Byron, and Willis. In July of 1830, Whittier eagerly accepted the editorship of another Clay organ, *The New England Weekly Review*, from George Prentice, its witty and urbane editor, who had previously corresponded with Whittier and praised his writings. The offer to manage one of New England's most respected journals must have seemed miraculous to Whittier, marooned as he had been by the death of his father on the Haverhill farm.

The following eighteen months as an editor in Hartford with its increasing responsibilities, wider social and literary contacts, and intense political atmosphere took its toll on Whittier's frail health. By the end of 1831, physically exhausted, he was forced to retire to the comparative seclusion of the farm where he must have dismally brooded on the disastrous finish to a prized editorial job. But if the end was bitter and frustrating, the journey had been of real benefit. Socially Whittier had been welcomed into the best homes and became a member of the cosmopolitan literary circle that revolved about Mrs. Sigourney, who was just then gaining recognition for her "Death of a Little Infant" and other poems which were to make her the most popular writer of pre-Civil War days. During his editorship he published over fifty poems,

many of them tinged with the rhapsodic emotionalism and diffuse sentimentality of the Hemans-Sigourney school. Also he
selected a group of his verse tales and prose sketches for his
first book, *Legends of New England* (1831). The collection
had only slight artistic merit—Whittier himself in later years
destroyed every copy he could find—but it was one of the first
attempts by a New England author to utilize native material.
The book revealed Whittier's intimate knowledge of local legend,
Colonial history, and folk superstition, as well as his responsive-
ness to native scenery and setting. Similarly, his long introduction to *The Literary Remains of John G. C. Brainard* (1832)
contained a shrewd insight into the real source of Brainard's
slight genius and indirectly indicated the path that he himself
needed to take:

> There is one important merit in his poetry which would redeem
> a thousand faults. It is wholly American. If he "Babbles o' green
> fields" and trees they are such as of right belong to us. He does not
> talk of palms and cypress where he should describe the rough oak
> and sombre hemlock. He prefers the lowliest blossom of Yankee-
> land to the gorgeous magnolia and orange bower of another clime.
> It is this which has made his poetry popular and his name dear
> in New-England.

However, Whittier's diminishing poetic output (only thirty-
eight poems in 1831 and 1832) attests to his growing dissatisfac-
tion with chances for poetic fame. Under the stimulus of a national election and the coming presidential campaign, Whittier
advocated the tariff, defended the U. S. Bank from the attacks
of Jackson, censured Calhoun's threat of nullification, and even
helped Prentice write a campaign biography of Clay. Throughout his editorship Whittier enthusiastically supported the manu-
facturing platform of Clay and doggedly railed at Jackson as one
"whose passions were his rulers, and whose love of country was
swallowed up in his supreme love of self." Experience brought
mastery of propaganda techniques and the art of caustic satire.
One would hardly recognize the mild Quaker boy of a few years
before in this slashing comment on a rival editor: "He cuts a sorry
figure it is true, but that is not the fault of Gideon [the editor].
The assinine [sic] propensities of a certain long-eared animal,
when brought upon the list ground of the noble war horse, are

always distinctly manifest in the light of contrast." His acid pen only whetted his appetite for politics, as did his constant exchanges with other eastern newspapers. Commenting and observing were no longer sufficient for he yearned to become a politician. In numerous letters to close friends Whittier self-importantly dramatizes his ill-health and political ambitions: "If my life is spared, the world shall know me in a loftier capacity than *as a writer of rhymes.*" Repeatedly he claims that "politics is the only field now open for me" and that he would have his fame now or not at all. Yet ill-health, his "hypo" tendency as he called it, did interfere and forced him to spend longer times away from his Hartford desk and finally to resign. This established a recurring pattern for him in the 1830's—a period of intense activity followed by a physical collapse.

At home his dominating interests continued to be political as he attended the state convention of the National Republican party, found a new political hero in Daniel Webster, and wrote violent articles attacking Jackson's bank veto. A local situation soon worked to his advantage. Caleb Cushing, the front-running Essex County candidate for Congress, had been unable to obtain the majority necessary for election. By 1832 he was willing to transfer his backing to someone who could unite the various factions within the Whig party, and Whittier was being considered. Since he was under the required age (he would be twenty-five in December), Whittier tried to foster a stalemate by playing one group against the other, thus prolonging the contest until he was able to accept the nomination. He even promised his friends political preference if he were elected. Although the stratagem failed, it showed how strongly Whittier wanted the office and to what lengths he would go to secure it. For once practical gain had blinded the Inner Light of his strict Quaker conscience. With this setback Whittier reached the bleak dead end of a road begun so auspiciously in 1827. Editorial positions had brought new friendships and mature responsibilities but no financial security or permanence; his poverty and Quaker background rendered him ineligible for the marriages he wanted; his poetry had achieved ephemeral newspaper fame, but his first book received no notice; and despite ill-health, he had the burden of managing the farm. The winter months of 1832–3 must have been depressing ones for Whittier, once again pondering the question of how to achieve success. Perhaps local politics would have been the answer, had not Whittier's alter ego, William Lloyd Garrison, again intervened. Though the two men had not corresponded regularly, Whittier's editorial comments on prison reform, temperance, Indian problems, rights of the laboring class, and the condition of slaves echoed Garrison's views. In 1830 while editing a paper in Baltimore Garrison had been briefly imprisoned for his fiery, untempered accusations against slave traders and Whittier had appealed to Clay for the bond money to obtain Garrison's release; a year later Whittier wrote a heartfelt tribute to Garrison, praising him for his "martyr's zeal" and "steadfast strength of truth" in fighting to free the slaves. During the spring of 1833 Garrison renewed their correspondence and specifically asked Whittier to consider the moral evil of slavery. Garrison pleaded: "This, then, is a time for the philanthropist—any friend of his country, to put forth his energies, in order to let the oppressed go free, and sustain the republic. The cause is worthy of Gabriel—yea, the God of hosts places himself at its head. Whittier enlist!—Your talents, zeal, influence—all are needed." Whether or not this appeal was the deciding factor in Whittier's turn to Abolition, it certainly cut to the core of Whittier's Quaker training on the sin of slavery and gave his susceptible, still undecided temperament a strength and directness of purpose for which it had been searching. During the next few months Whittier studied all the existing material on Colonization and slavery that he could obtain and in June published *Justice and Expediency* to herald his entrance into the Abolitionist party.

❧ ☙

Since the next twenty years engulfed the poet in a welter of antislavery writing and in the turmoil of practical politics, an evaluation of his poetic accomplishment up to 1833 should be taken. As Whitman Bennett has phrased it, "If ever a man learned to drive nails by swinging a hammer, Whittier learned to write poetry by writing it." During these apprenticeship years, Whittier wrote a staggering total of over two hundred and eighty poems, a number equal to his entire output in the next thirty years. Whittier disparaged his early verse as "wretched first appearances" and fought bitterly to have them excluded from his collected works. Still they afford a valuable glimpse into the interests, methods, and development of the young writer. Many of these early poems teach moral lessons by paraphrasing familiar psalms or dramatizing crucial moments from scripture. Others also reflect his religious background, dealing with the customs, traditions, and martyrs of the Quaker faith. But in the main, the English Romantics and their American counterparts furnished the themes and literary models for Whittier.

The lure of the exotic and the mysterious captured his young imagination and, like thousands of Americans, Whittier responded to the excitement occasioned by Scott's stirring tales. Scores of Whittier's poems imitated Scott's historical approach with his emphasis on battles, romantic interludes, thrilling rescues, and virtuous heroes. A typical example of Whittier's dressing his Indians "in Sir Walter Scott's plaid" and his bookish approach to native material is "The Pawnee Brave." The plot tells of the rescue of an Indian girl by her Pawnee lover and is embellished by a brooding Gothic atmosphere of suspense and mystery:

> Grimly towards the clouded skies,
> Gleamed the fire of sacrifice,
> On the mist-encumbered air,
> Widely flashed the baleful glare;
> Swiftly down its rugged bed,
> Rolled the torrent darkly red.

This extravagant, stereotyped diction continues with Whittier's description of the girl surrounded by "the horrid laugh, and fiendish yell." The following passage echoes the popular declamatory style of Scott's martial poems and even copies the conventional heroic simile:

> Will they [the Indian warriors] from their purpose stay?
> Will the dance of death delay?
> Sooner from its destined bourne,
> Shall the mountain torrent turn;
> Sooner shall the whirlwind's wrath
>   Pause in desolation's path.

Although Whittier tried to imitate Scott and others, Lord Byron, the symbol of the romantic ego and the adventurous spirit, claimed his most ardent attention. Whittier criticized Byron's amoral life and feared his "licentious" poetry, but was fascinated by his investigation of the passions and psychological handling of sin and rebellion. For over ten years Whittier's poetry and prose mirrored aspects of the Byronic hero's cynicism and disillusionment. Since these pieces drew on sentiments quite foreign to Whittier's Quaker simplicity and New England common sense, their posturizing and attempted sophistication rendered them artificial and unconvincing. Along with this Byronic melancholy Whittier absorbed the sentimentality and pietism of Mrs. Hemans and her American followers, Mrs. Sigourney and N. P. Willis. These writers taught generalized ethical lessons by exploring such diverse subjects as the deaths of small infants, menaced virtue, the loss of a prized ring, the joys of motherhood, and the beauty of a city pigeon. A delicate refinement and excessive concern for propriety saved their verses from the least hint of vulgarity or realism. Even in her autobiography Mrs. Sigourney avoided the distressing word "hog" by calling it "a quadruped member of our establishment." She is representative of the host of pre-Civil War newspaper versifiers and gift book writers whose trite moralizing, diffuse rhapsodic style, and vague unrestrained imagery corrupted American popular taste. "The Declaration" is a good example of Whittier's sentimental verse in this manner. The poet describes himself as having fallen hopelessly in love with a beauty who ignores his devotion. Whittier portrays her charms by the conventional phrases that Mrs. Sigourney was so fond of: the blush over her fair cheek is "a pearl and coral fellowship" and her "form of grace" and "waving hair" are recalled in a sentimental half-forgotten dream. Whittier addresses the girl as "holy light," "pure, bright star of even," and "radiant sphere"; and finally he sums up his despair with an elaborate comparison of his unrequited love to the pagan who prays in vain to nonexistent gods:

> And mine shall be the ungentle task
>   To love—when love can only be
> Like one who bows him down in prayer
>   Before some veiled and mystic shrine,
> Even when the idol-glories there,
>   May never on his worship shine!

Throughout the poem love is treated in this affected literary way with stilted language and outlandish imagery. Fortunately, imitating Sigourney and Willis was only a passing fad; but Whittier's continued use of the Byronic hero and attempts to rival Scott's narrative romances showed how impressionable and uncertain his taste was. His lack of critical discernment and his newspaper-fed diet of poor verse prevented him from distinguishing between dullness and inspiration. The want of revision, careless use of language, and uneven versification and rhyme in these early poems continued to plague his mature work; while the themes of lost love, melancholy, and poetic fame indicate how far Whittier had come from the homespun songs of Burns and the Quaker belief that art must be practical and moral. One of the main tensions in his literary career is again placed in focus: the lure of beauty in its own sphere and a moralistic view of literature which relegates beauty to a secondary position.

In the main, Whittier's writing up to 1833 with the break occasioned by his entrance into Abolition reveals three formative influences: his religious training which led him to consider literature from an ethical viewpoint; his isolated rural background and Burns's poetry which influenced him to seek poetic material within his own environment and experience; and finally the romantic verse of Scott and Byron which taught him the value of affections, while the sentimental traits of their American imitators fashioned his literary style. One notes in particular the wide variety of conflicting influences acting on Whittier and the uncertainty of his own views on the function of literature. Though he could clearly see the faults of the diluted Byronic verse of Willis, he continued to imitate him; though he ridiculed the implausible stories of Cooper and his lack of characterization, he committed worse sins in his own poetry and prose; and though he believed morality to be the basis of literature, he ignored this tenet in many of his verses. The number of literary experiments that Whittier made in seeking the right medium for expressing his genius is surprising too: the poetic prose of Ossian, the Scottish dialect of Burns, the "awful grandeur" of Byron, the graveyard approach of Mrs. Sigourney, and the dilettantish love poetry of Willis. The year 1833 found Whittier still searching and the essential truth that he had once seen in Burns's poetry appeared lost forever.

3

∽§ ABOLITIONIST ACTIVITY

IN AN autobiographical section of "The Tent on the Beach,"
Whittier states that his Abolitionist interests made him one

> Who, with a mission to fulfil,
> Had left the Muses' haunts to turn
> The crank of an opinion-mill,
> Making his rustic reed of song
> A weapon in the war with wrong,
> Yoking his fancy to the breaking-plough
> That beam-deep turned the soil for truth to
> spring and grow.
>
> .   .   .   .
>
> A silent, shy, peace-loving man,
> He seemed no fiery partisan
> To hold his way against the public frown,
> The ban of Church and State, the fierce
> mob's hounding down.

These quiet, moving lines barely indicate the profound emotional
and moral transformation that took place once Whittier had
written *Justice and Expediency.* For the next twenty years his
life was written on the pages of American history with William
Lloyd Garrison, John Quincy Adams, Daniel Webster, Charles

Sumner, and others. He helped form the protest Liberty party
in 1840 and assisted its merger into the powerful Free-Soil party
which in turn formed the nucleus for the Republican party. His
single-minded dedication to the Abolitionist cause effectively
"vetoed poetry" and converted the romantic young lyricist into
master propagandist. Whittier's full commitment to Abolition
was sealed by the relentlessly phrased arguments in *Justice and
Expediency*. The pamphlet demonstrated the failure of the Colonization society and contended that immediate emancipation
was "a safe and just peaceful remedy for the evils of the slave
system" and that "free labor, its necessary consequence, is more
productive, and more advantageous to the planter than slave
labor." Though the paper expounded widely accepted logical and
moral principles, its underlying concepts of universal suffrage and
elimination of slavery seemed dangerous to northern businessmen
and heretical and Union-destroying to southern slaveowners. Actually, the publication of *Justice and Expediency* destroyed Whittier's hopes for political preferment, severely limited the number
of reviews and journals which dared to publish his verse, and
earned him a notoriety that was exceeded only by popular hatred
for Garrison. For distributing this pamphlet in Washington, Dr.
Reuben Crandall was arrested, imprisoned for eight months, and
finally tried for "circulating seditious and incendiary papers."
Although he was acquitted, the doctor died two years later of con-
sumption which he had contracted while in prison. A few months
after the publication of the pamphlet Whittier served as secretary
for the National Anti-Slavery convention and helped frame its
declaration of sentiments which essentially sounded the death knell
for slavery by its moral insistence on universal emancipation and
full social equality for Negroes.

From the beginning Whittier realized the difficulties and problems of getting the Abolitionist platform accepted and realistically
estimated that his own political skill would be an effective weapon.
As Bliss Perry noted in his sketch of Whittier:

> His judgment was canny. His knowledge of local conditions, at
> first in his native town and county, and afterward throughout
> New England and the Eastern states, was singularly exact. He
> seemed to perceive, as by some actual visualization, how people
> were thinking and feeling in Massachusetts, Connecticut, Penn-
> sylvania, and other communities which he had observed at first

hand. . . . Men were never abstractions to him. They were concrete persons, with ambitions to be tempted, generosities to be
wakened, weaknesses to be utilized. His own county of Essex was
then, as now, noted for the adroitness of its politicians, but at
twenty-five John Greenleaf Whittier could beat the best of them
at their own game.

In public and political action Whittier took men as they were,
neither "saints [n]or angels," and was willing to lobby, com-
promise, and shift to obtain necessary votes. Instinctively he
recognized that moral action apart from political effort was an
absurdity. His belief in the ideal never obscured the practical
problems of its realization as it did for Garrison and other hard-
core Abolitionists. His maneuvering with congressman Caleb
Cushing is a classic example of political manipulation. To obtain
his election Cushing had to pledge support of Abolitionist petitions opposing slavery. In 1838 when Cushing attempted to
repudiate his promise, Whittier so effectively swung the votes in
his district that Cushing was forced to write an open letter indicating his continued support of Abolitionist aims. By 1840
Cushing felt so politically secure that he again broke his pledge
and was elected. With the national Whig triumph Cushing was to
be rewarded for his party efforts with the nomination as Secretary of the Treasury, but Whittier quietly had the letter of
1838 circulated and Cushing's nomination was defeated.

With similar tenacity Whittier badgered congressional leaders
such as Clay and Webster with letters about their antislavery
sentiments and repeatedly urged Lowell, Longfellow, and Emerson to enlist themselves on the Abolitionists' side. Finally Whittier's assistance helped John Quincy Adams in his fight against
the infamous Gag rule, which prohibited all petitions dealing with
slavery in the District of Columbia. Whittier edited Adams'
letters and undoubtedly wrote a part of the Haverhill Petition
of 1842. This grimly ironic document countered the continual
southern threat of secession by asking for a northern withdrawal
since so much favoritism was shown the South. In the tumult
that followed, Adams himself barely escaped expulsion from the
House for submitting the petition and insulting the American
people. Now the Abolitionist fight was widened beyond the
crazed efforts of a few fanatics to free the slaves—it involved
the universal rights of all men to the freedoms of press and

speech. Throughout this period, after one brief term in the Massachusetts House of Representatives, Whittier was a well-known lobbyist at the state house in Boston. As the leader of the Abolitionist faction, he had "caucused in season and out of season, threatened and coaxed, plead [sic] and scolded," until he had forced the House to pass a resolution censuring President Van Buren's attempt to stop antislavery discussion. He opened his editorship of the *Essex Gazette* in May of 1836 with the ringing statement, "I regard the present struggle as the closing one between Liberty and Slavery in this republic." So vehemently did he espouse the Abolitionist cause that he was reduced to a junior editor in September and indignantly resigned in December. In 1837 he was in New York working with the leading Abolitionists and the next year became editor of the *Pennsylvania Freeman,* one of the leading antislavery papers in the North. Now nearly all his poetry dealt with the slave problem as Whittier became his party's finest propagandist.

The 1830's were the most physically trying of Whittier's life. He traveled all over the North, attending conventions, lobbying, cajoling votes, even publicly speaking in an effort to win support for the Abolitionist cause. Repeatedly he was caught in mob action. In September, 1835, while traveling with George Thompson, a noted British Abolitionist speaker, Whittier was assaulted with rocks and debris by a Concord, New Hampshire, mob who wanted to tar and feather Thompson. Whittier received only slight injuries and both he and Thompson managed to escape. Weeks later he witnessed the attempted lynching of Garrison by a Boston mob. Even in his own Essex County Whittier was pelted with stones while attending an antislavery meeting in Newburyport. His most dangerous brush came in 1838 when the newly dedicated Pennsylvania Hall, erected under Abolitionist auspices, was destroyed and burned by a surging mob of fifteen thousand. Disguised in a wig and long white overcoat, Whittier mingled with the crowd and managed to save some personal possessions while his office was being sacked. Freedom was proving a hard taskmaster. The strain of constant editorial duties, growing political activity, and finally mob violence brought on so serious a physical breakdown in 1840 that his doctors feared permanent injury. Whittier resigned as editor and returned to his new home in Amesbury. This scare, followed by others, apparently taught

Whittier to husband his meagre strength, for he gradually lessened his active reform work. His ill-health imprisoned him in Amesbury, where he worked for the remainder of his life. He could never write continuously for even a half-hour without severe head pains and a few months of any editorial job seemed all he could endure. Henceforth the world had to come to him, for he was never again to leave the comparative isolation and protective bond of his family home; nor was he ever to marry.

At this time Whittier met the two women who most deeply stirred his emotional nature. In 1837 while working in Brooklyn Whittier befriended a young poetess, Lucy Hooper. Her Essex County background and her appealing youth—she was only twenty—as well as her intense interest in Abolition and her delicate poetic talent affected Whittier and their attachment was so close that by 1839 they were considered engaged. Undoubtedly they considered marriage, but again lack of money and Whittier's dedication to his work, coupled with Lucy's ailing health, presented insurmountable obstacles. She died prematurely in 1841.

During his editorship of the *Pennsylvania Freeman,* Whittier met Elizabeth Lloyd, "the most beautiful woman he ever saw." A poised social conversationalist, an ardent Abolitionist, an aspiring poetess, and a Quakeress besides, she was a striking combination of physical beauty and intelligence. After Lucy Hooper's death their friendship grew, but, when she archly began to chide Whittier for his coldness and to beg that he visit her, Whittier retreated and no romantic responses answered her whimsical flirting. Eventually she married, in 1853, but was soon widowed and by 1858 Whittier was regularly seeing her in Philadelphia. The former attraction was now strengthened by her recent loss and Whittier's own sorrow over the death of his mother. A series of openly ardent letters during 1858 and 1859 traces the development of a mature love. Whittier could tell her not to write to him if it hurt her eyes for "the very blank papers which thy hand has folded for my sake will be dear to me." After returning from a visit in May, 1859, Whittier wrote: "Elizabeth, I have been happy far more so than I ever expected in this life. The sweet memory of the past few weeks makes me rich forever. What Providence has in store for the future I know not—I dare not hope scarcely,—but the past is mine—may I not say ours—

26

sacred and beautiful, a joy forever. Asking nothing of thee, and with tenderest regard for thy grief and memories I have given thee what was thine by right—the love of an honest heart." Yet the years of bachelorhood would not so easily be ignored; his personal reticence about emotional feelings, his cautious fears about marriage, his own precarious health, and his insecure financial position again proved too strong. Almost as if amazed at his own ardor, Whittier wrote in August, tactfully breaking off their plans. for marriage:

> I have grown old in a round of duties and responsibilities which still govern me and urge me: my notions of life and daily habits are old-fashioned and homely. . . . I cannot, dear E., be blind to the fact that thee lives in a different sphere—that thy sense of the fitting and beautiful demand accessories and surroundings very different from those that have become familiar and habitual to me. I am sure thy fine artist-nature would pine and die under the hard and uncongenial influences that make me what I am, and from which I cannot escape without feeling that I have abandoned the post of duty, without losing my self respect, and forfeiting all right to be loved in return by those I love.

❧ ☙

His forced return to home roots had noticeable effects. If it defeated his hopes for national leadership in a now powerful Liberty party, it gave him the detachment and perspective necessary to write better Abolitionist poetry. If it removed him from the social attractions of Philadelphia and his incipient romantic interest in Elizabeth Lloyd, it caused him to again seek diversion in native scenery and legend. His new ballads and nature pieces showed his reawakened pleasure in "the unsung beauty hid [below] life's common things." Finally, if it again thwarted his innermost ambitions, it occasioned a searching self-appraisal of his aims and goals which led him back to the strength of his Quaker heritage. For the first time Whittier understood the full significance of the Inner Light. After one meeting of the Friends, Whittier experienced a peculiar manifestation of the power and personal application of this doctrine. One of the Quakers, Richard Mott, asked to accompany Whittier home. "During our walk," Whittier records, "he told me he knew not how it was or why, but that his mind had been drawn into a deep and extraordinary

Whittier's Home at Amesbury, Massachusetts

exercise of sympathy with me; that he had been sensible of a deep trial and exercise in my own mind; that he had felt it so strongly that he could not rest easy without informing me of it, although he had heard nothing and seen nothing to produce this conviction in his mind. . . . I confess I was startled . . . its personal application to myself in a manner so inexplicable by merely human reasoning awed me." A later letter to Mott indicates Whittier's realistic awareness of his need for spiritual guidance: "My temperament, ardent, impetuous, imaginative, powerfully acted upon from without, keenly susceptible to all influences from the intellectual world, as well as to those of nature, in her varied manifestations, is, I fear, ill adapted to that quiet, submissive, introverted state of patient and passive waiting for direction and support under these trials and difficulties." A group of poems questioning the nature of man's relationship with God, written in the 1840's, also reveal his gradual and deepening confidence in the will of God. At last Whittier was achieving the spiritual assurance and mental harmony necessary for full maturity and artistic achievement.

Though as personally dedicated to the Abolitionist cause as the most rabid of Garrison's followers, Whittier knew that only by broadening their political appeal could the Abolitionists gain popular support. Whittier's willingness to tack with empirical winds and his insistence on political action irritated Garrison's idealistic nature. Garrison preferred disunion to a continued endurance of slavery. He persisted in advocating other sectarian reforms which limited the Abolitionists' appeal to independent voters. Their continued disagreement on procedure so rankled Garrison that he openly accused Whittier of trying to obtain peace "at the expense of consistency, if not of principle." And when Whittier finally resigned from the *Pennsylvania Freeman* in 1840, Garrison caustically remarked that at one time Whittier's retirement would have occasioned regret "but in his present state of mind, as it respects political action . . . we are reconciled to his withdrawal." The choice between retaining Garrison's personal friendship or following his own course was a difficult one for Whittier, but he now threw his weight behind the new Abolitionist splinter group to help form the Liberty party. The break was complete when Whittier actively campaigned for Congress in 1842 and was accused by Garrison and his followers of betraying the cause. Eventually the Liberty party joined the Free-Soilers as a national third party organization which helped swing the balance of power by the 1848 elections.

Though diminishing his personal participation in the Abolitionist cause, Whittier remained poet laureate for the Liberty party, and his indignation rang out over the annexation of Texas and the Mexican War. In 1844 Whittier edited a new Liberty party organ, *The Middlesex Standard,* and passionately pleaded for the election of James Birney as President over Whittier's former political mentor, Clay, whom he now characterized as "the man who had done *more than any other man now living to extend and perpetrate slavery.*" By 1848 he was corresponding editor for the *National Era,* the most influential of all Abolitionist papers, and for the next ten years its columns contained the best of Whittier's prose and poetry.

Whittier's most singular political feat lay before him, however

—the drafting of Charles Sumner for the United States Senate in 1850. They had become acquainted in the late 1840's through exchanges of antislavery sentiments. As a graduate of Harvard with an acceptable social background, Sumner's oratorical ability and reform sympathies made him a much sought after political candidate, but it was Whittier alone who finally persuaded Sumner to run for the Senate on the Free-Soil ticket. By a shrewd political maneuver, Whittier's Free-Soil party agreed to vote for a Democratic governor against Whig opposition if the Democrats in turn would support Sumner for the Senate. Although the Democrats later recanted, Sumner was elected. Throughout his term of office Sumner maintained a trenchant antislavery position and Whittier continued to advise him. When Sumner was struck down and badly injured after his violent "The Crime Against Kansas" tirade, an emotionally roused North cried for blood. Writing about the incident, Whittier not only took a broader perspective but fully expressed his political credo:

> It seems to me to be no time for the indulgence of mere emotions. Neither railing nor threats befit the occasion. It is our first duty to inquire, why it is that the bad men in power have been emboldened to commit the outrages of which we complain. Why is it that the South has dared to make such experiments upon us. The North is not united for freedom, as the South is for slavery. . . . The one indispensible thing for us is Union. Can we not have it? Can we not set an example in this very neighborhood,—Whigs, Democrats, Free-Soilers, and Americans, joining hands in defense of our common liberties? We must forget, forgive, and UNITE.

But even Whittier was not immune to the violent passions swirling about him and repeatedly his shocked indignation over the North's compromises expressed itself in stirring political verse that belied his Quaker hope for peace. From Webster's "Seventh of March" (1850) speech for conciliation came Whittier's terrible denunciation of the betrayal, "Ichabod"; the bloody fighting in Kansas occasioned "The Kansas Emigrants," "Le Marais du Cygne," and "Letter . . ."; while the arrest of fugitive slaves and his hatred for church hypocrisy brought forth "Moloch in State Street" and "Official Piety." When war became inevitable, Whittier sadly perceived the bitter end of his reform efforts and wondered momentarily if perhaps disunion weren't better than a civil war. Yet, when war came, he defended Lincoln's position and fully indicated what the passive Quakers must do: "We have no right to ask or expect an exemption . . . we owe it to the cause of truth, to show that exalted heroism and generous self-sacrifice are not incompatible with our pacific principles. Our mission is, at this time, to mitigate the sufferings of our countrymen, to visit and aid the sick and the wounded, to relieve the necessities of the widow and orphan, and to practice economy for the sake of charity."

After the election of Sumner, Whittier gradually turned to writing home legends and ballads. The twenty years had taken their toll, and a weary Whittier asked for mental rest, saying "I have crowded into a few years what should have been given to many." Yet, the struggle had far-reaching personal effects and important literary consequences. The vilification and mob abuse, the ostracism from literary life, the bitter break with Garrison had toughened Whittier's mild Quaker soul and had given him hard-won knowledge of fickle human nature. His dedicated absorption in a moral cause had purified and refined all the dross of earlier posturizing, and the swirl of practical politics and unscrupulous ambition about him had intensified his regard for eternal standards and the consolation of the Inner Light. During these years Whittier had written mainly Abolitionist and political verses. Later he admitted that they were written "with no expectation that they would survive the occasions which called them forth: they were protests, alarm signals, trumpet-calls to action, words wrung from the writer's heart, forged at white heat, and of course lacking . . . finish and careful word-selection." Certainly Whittier was right, for most of them were artistic failures, but they did bring important gains for the mature poet. Their passion and intensity strengthened and reforged the vapid sentimental verses of his formative years. The Abolitionist movement drew Whittier away from a love of poetry by itself to a universal awareness of man's spiritual significance, his need for love and respect, and his hunger for freedom. Expressing the poet's innermost belief in the power of the human will to overcome evil and his emotional response to slavery as a symbol of all oppression—physical, economic, or spiritual, these poems aroused an immediate popular response by substituting emotional feeling for the logic and dryness of political appeal. Often his verses were printed in broadsides and distributed by the thousands throughout the country.

Some were accompanied by woodcut pictures in much the same manner as World War I atrocity posters. For example, "Our Countrymen in Chains" depicts a chained Negro on his knees raising his manacled hands to heaven asking, "Am I not a man and brother?" These poems furnish an interesting insight into the nature of propaganda: the attempt to mold public opinion by capitalizing on the popular appeal and excitement of dramatic contemporary events.

❧ ☙

"The Sabbath Scene" illustrates his striving for sensational details to excite and move the reader. Growing out of Whittier's concern about the effects of the Fugitive Slave Act, the poem scathingly mocks the clergy's use of the Bible to justify the law. It tells in the best Harriet B. Stowe manner of the "wasted female figure," who rushes into a church meeting ("like a scared fawn before the hounds"), pursued by the vicious "lank-haired hunter," whip in hand. Her appeal fails to move the minister, and he orders his deacon to "throw that Polyglott/Before the wench, and trip her!" Then comes the climax:

> Plump dropped the holy tome, and o'er
>   Its sacred pages stumbling,
> Bound hand and foot, a slave once more,
>   The hapless wretch lay trembling.

The picture of the girl being tripped by the Bible was undoubtedly meant as biting satire on the misuse of religion, but the image of the Bible catching a girl who had already stopped fleeing and who was surrounded by scores of people is absurd rather than tragic. Also the phrasing throughout is unfortunate: the rhyming of "whip her" with "trip her" jars the ear, while the circumlocutions of "Polyglott" and "tome" remind one of Mrs. Sigourney's euphuisms. The poet's response to this outlandish scene is the best section in the poem:

> "Is this." I cried,
> "The end of prayer and preaching?
> Then down with pulpit, down with priest,
>   And give us Nature's teaching!"

In the final stanzas Whittier's blazing moral indignation is communicated simply and directly. Precisely because the narrative was sensational, the imagery unrestrained and cliché-ridden, and the entire situation melodramatic and crude, the poem had tremendous popular success. It was issued in broadsides, widely copied in northern newspapers, and even published as a separate pamphlet. Also its portrayal of the terrible results of the new law accurately foreshadowed occurrences every bit as unbelievable as the one presented in the poem. Though clearly showing the faults of hasty composition and uncontrolled feeling, the poem displays Whittier's competent handling of ballad meter and sense of narrative pace.

⋙ ⋘

An earlier Abolitionist poem, "Massachusetts to Virginia," was occasioned by the Boston trial of an escaped Virginia slave. The poem's sweeping hexameters and patterned rhetorical movement perfectly fitted popular oratory and it was widely recited. In it Whittier invokes Massachusetts' pride in her various political and social freedoms to lash Virginia for denying these basic democratic tenets. He contrasts Virginia's present position with that of Washington and Jefferson, recalling the brotherhood of the two states during the Revolutionary War. The core of the poem, Massachusetts' condemnation of Virginia for betraying her democratic heritage, is introduced by a brief survey of Massachusetts' free sailors, fishermen, farmers, and lumberjacks. This is followed by a catalogue of individual communities, responding to Virginia's threats. The detailed knowledge of local traits and specific sectional qualities swells the list into a powerful panoramic view of Massachusetts' unified strength. The climax of "No fetters in the Bay State! No slave upon her land" echoes the cry of all men for freedom. Here the plea is based on sound historical knowledge and intimate association with the districts named, and the presentation is concrete and realistic, imaginatively creating the atmosphere of the individual sections. Nor does the rhetorical movement of the poem mar its validity as a deep-felt expression of the rights of all men to be free.

⋙ ⋘

Whittier's increasing reliance on his own territory as the medium for his thoughts and the source of his imagery fused with his historical knowledge and humanitarian interests to pro-

33

duce some of his better ballads. Taking tales of old Quaker fighters for liberty in "The Exiles" and "Barclay of Ury" or simple accounts of free laboring men, Whittier began to transmute the rough ore of the commonplace into valuable artistic metal. Also his seclusion in Amesbury opened the floodgates of memory—of the simple rural boyhood, the wholesome farm activities, and the local superstitions and legends. As the mood of nostalgia and recollection deepened, Whittier was ready for his most characteristic and enduring verse.

At the same time Whittier was writing his best prose. In 1845 he collected a series of articles and published *The Stranger in Lowell;* and from his association with the *National Era* came nearly three hundred prose pieces, including his one success in fiction, *Margaret Smith's Journal,* and almost all the essays and literary sketches that he included in his collected prose works. These articles, reminiscences, and fictional pieces show a similar development of interest in the past Colonial days, in "charms and fairy faith," and in the values of simple farm life. In an essay on Robert Dinsmore, Whittier comments: "We have no songs; American domestic life has never been hallowed and beautified by the sweet and graceful and tender associations of poetry. We have no Yankee pastorals. Our rivers and streams turn mills and float rafts, and are otherwise as commendably useful as those of Scotland; but no quaint ballad or simple song reminds us that men and women have loved, met, and parted on their banks, or that beneath each roof within their valleys the tragedy and comedy of life have been enacted." This lack Whittier himself was soon to supply. By the 1850's Whittier had finished the best of his prose works, as he had completed his main reform efforts. Now all was ready for the poet to emerge after his long hibernation. His ill-paid, physically exhausting dedication to moral principles was about to return the proverbially hundredfold. The death of the reformer marked the birth of the poet.

4

✑ POETIC MATURITY

WHITTIER once whimsically remarked, "My vehicles have been of the humbler sort—merely the farm wagon and buckboard of verse. . . . I shall not dare to warrant any of my work for a long drive." This was Whittier's achievement—to have represented the common thoughts and feelings of a mainly agrarian society. Whittier wrote with his age's strong moral sense and its complete confidence in progress and democratic concepts. Hardly a profound thinker, Whittier remained like his readers strikingly unaware of the vast social and economic changes in the nineteenth century and only superficially understood that Abolition alone was no panacea for his age's ills. Nevertheless, he did have a tenacious grasp on a few fundamentals: farm life, nature, moral principles, freedom, and the Inner Light. If these realities were a narrow vein of poetic ore and mined to near exhaustion, their constant sifting and refining did produce a few finished poems.

✑ ❧

Whittier's poetic maturity came late—in his fifties and sixties—when his best work supposedly lay behind him. Few, if any, critics in the 1840's differed with Lowell's comments that Whittier's reform efforts had obscured his lyric gift and that his best poems

35

were "those . . . struck off at white-heats/When the heart in his breast like a triphammer beats." But in his mature work all the strands of his life were woven upon the loom of memory and reminiscence to furnish material for his finest poetry. So, from his farm rearing with its simple pleasures and hard work, from his Quaker belief in social equality and inner spirituality, from his battle for the slaves and all the oppressed, and from his love of Colonial New England came poems such as "Abraham Davenport," "Skipper Ireson's Ride," "Maud Muller," "Telling the Bees," "The Last Walk in Autumn," and "Snow-Bound."

Whittier's farm experience and rural boyhood with its resulting understanding and love of nature furnished the main themes for the mature poet. All natural beauty—the streams and fields of Haverhill, the trees and flowers along the Merrimack—attracted Whittier and was further valued because the Divine Creator was its source. But unlike the ardent Romantic writers whose love of nature's external beauty became an end in itself, or the transcendentalists who often regarded nature as a direct manifestation of the Divine, Whittier, as he wrote in "The Meeting," feared that nature

> . . . will not leave our senses still,
> But drags them captive at her will:
> And, making earth too great for heaven,
> She hides the Giver in the given.

Though he did enjoy the romantic and picturesque aspects of nature, he mainly appreciated its restful and healing qualities, finding in nature a refuge from the problems of life. Like Burns, Whittier usually associated nature with the simple joys of home. The most striking sunset or mountain vista paled when compared with the inner beauty of conscience and man's honest emotions. So a moral view dominated his response to nature as it ruled his life in other ways. Of course Whittier drew heavily on nature and his farm experience for imagery and pictorial description, but mainly this background furnished him with certain basic concepts—the value of hard work and rural simplicity, nature's role as a teacher of moral virtues—which were never absent from his verse.

A poem such as "Mabel Martin" exemplifies his usual approach and characteristic views. The carefully set introduction exactly describes the Merrimack valley and graphically renders its quiet appeal with a pictorial skill that was so peculiarly Whittier's:

> Across the level tableland,
>   A grassy, rarely trodden way,
>   With thinnest skirt of birchen spray
>
> And stunted growth of cedar, leads
>   To where you see the dull plain fall
>   Sheer off, steep-slanted, ploughed by all
>
> The season's rainfalls. On its brink
>   The over-leaning harebells swing,
>   With roots half bare the pine-trees cling.

However, Whittier interrupts his scenic description to praise the crops of the section, the modest homesteads, and rough farmers who stand "ground-fast in their native fields,/Untempted by the city's gain." This concept occurs repeatedly in Whittier's poetry— the inherent value of farm life which emphasizes hard work, instills wholesome simplicity and moral values, and orders nature's wild beauty into vineyards and fields of wheat. The city is presented as mechanized and cruelly indifferent, hiding poverty and dissipation beneath its glittering facade.

The story proper opens with an account of a harvest night in the "dim colonial time/Of sterner lives and gloomier faith":

> It was the pleasant harvest-time,
>   When cellar-bins are closely stowed,
>   And garrets bend beneath their load,
>
> And the old swallow-hunted barns,—
>   Brown-gabled, long, and full of seams
>   Through which the moted sunlight streams.

The ensuing scene pictures the rude tales, hearty games, and simple actions of "sun-embrowned" boys and of "pastoral Ruth(s)" waiting for the "red-ear's kiss of forfeiture," while introducing an outcast from this happiness, Mabel Martin. Her ostracism, as the daughter of a witch, was based on the actual history of Susanna Martin who was the only woman hanged for witchcraft north of the Merrimack River. Shunned and taunted as she sits alone at the husking, the girl returns in tears to her deserted home. However, her pathetic situation wins the love of an older farmer who forces the villagers to accept her as his wife and checks their superstitious fears. The triumph of love in this poem despite the obstacles of his age and her youth, his social position and her disreputable background, and his gruffness and her beauty was one of Whittier's favorite themes: that no caste or social distinction would ever separate true love.

Similarly, in "Among the Hills" the simple farmer wins the sophisticated city girl in a perfect blend of "culture's charm and labor's strength"; in "Amy Wentworth" the beautiful heiress of wealth and tradition defies her family to wait for a lowborn sea captain, for "love has never known a law"; and in "The Countess" a visiting French nobleman finds true happiness in his marriage to a simple village girl, who blends her "sweet unconsciousness" with his culture and position. These poems of domestic love and idyllic marriage too closely reflect Longfellow's genteel handling of similar themes to be artistically satisfying. Yet in "Snow-Bound" Whittier makes these same domestic emotions as valid and realistic as the farmhouse he describes, by using the wood fire to symbolize the bond of family love, by contrasting this love with the elemental forces of storm and night, and by remaining scrupulously faithful to the actual scene. Though these ideas are often naive and romantic, their main emphasis—the security of a past rural culture where such a harmony of ideal and practice did exist—has significance. Hidden beneath many of these farm idylls is the subconscious knowledge that the past, not the present, is the only place for such dreams. If Whittier did view farm life nostalgically and even sentimentally, he was aware also of the numberless poverty-stricken houses then existing in New England, pictured in his "Prelude" to "Among the Hills" with their

> Shrill, querulous women, sour and sullen men,
> Untidy, loveless, old before their time,
> With scarce a human interest save their own
> Monotonous round of small economies.

If he usually concentrated on optimistic prospects, it was not through ignorance. All of Whittier's mature poems expressed a belief in the inherent goodness of man who can, if stirred, reform his own evil tendencies and eradicate injustice and oppression. Whittier deeply believed that "there is little of actual suffering which may not be traced to intemperance, idleness, and utter lack of economy." Such a social platform did, as Pollard points out in his biography, "set too large a store by faith and reason; took altogether too little into account the driving power of the profit motive upon human conduct. . . . (and) the fact of economic class warfare." Still, Whittier's utter sincerity and almost mystical belief in the power of moral righteousness command respect. His few poetical triumphs were popular equivalents of Thoreau's deathless plea in *Walden* for "simplicity, simplicity, simplicity."

ಆ§ ೄ

Perhaps no other American poet was so extremely devoted to the concepts of freedom and the basic principles of democracy. Scores of his poems reiterate the need for proper voting, the moral responsibility of political leaders, the protection of minority rights, the freedom of press and speech, the ethical conscience in everyday life. Most of these poems are artistic failures, but occasionally his burning democratic convictions produced an "Ichabod," a "Laus Deo," or a "Massachusetts to Virginia" that compensates for the long spaces of dullness in his labor and reform poems. In his best poems these basic moral beliefs are neither platitudinous nor sentimental, but refreshingly direct and certain in a modern relativistic age.

Another aspect of his mature poetry is his use of history, legend, and folklore to vitalize his ideas on intolerance, personal dignity, moral courage, and reform. As he says in "The Garrison of Cape Ann," his tales were often written to give

> . . . far, faint glimpses of the dual life of old,
> Inward, grand with awe and reverence; outward, mean and coarse and cold;
> Gleams of mystic beauty playing over dull and vulgar clay.

Whittier's nostalgic recalling of these past times was an attempt to save a tradition and to record the passing of a social order. He clearly saw the interrelation of past and present and reverenced "whatever is good and true and heroic in the past, not because it is old, but because it brings with it the freshness and newness of an immortal life, and it is not merely a part of the past, but of the present [and] future also." And often these ballads and legends furnished insights for the present age.

Once Whittier's Abolitionist work was completed his poetry

increasingly stressed the need for inner reform, hinting at his own final understanding of the hollowness of social reform without a corresponding sense of moral responsibility in the individual. The Quaker belief in the personal indwelling of the Holy Spirit dominates his writings from 1870 onward. Whittier felt strongly that true religion rises above set creed and dogma and includes a non-denominational acceptance of the Bible and an unselfish love of neighbor. In fact Whittier believed, as he wrote in "My Soul and I," that

> Thy neighbor's wrong is thy present hell,
> His bliss, thy heaven.

The humanitarian and moral impulse that directed his Abolitionist work now led him to explore the mysteries of immortality, God's love, the nature of worship, the meaning of faith, and above all the mystical presence within one's own soul. Continually Whittier emphasizes his complete confidence in the mercy and love of God and his utter submission to the eternal will. Existing evil is caused by man's actions and what remains unexplainable has to be accepted on faith. This belief, strengthened by years of practical activity in an idealless world, expressed itself in religious verses that have remained America's most popular hymns. Whittier bypassed the complexities of good and evil coexisting in the world, preferring to trust that God will measure the good a man hopes to attain rather than judge his failures. Still Whittier did not completely ignore the problem, for his poems recognize the tragedy of man who has free will and who can accept or reject God's grace. His religious optimism was tempered by his knowledge that spiritual success comes only through suffering and pain and individual striving. As serene old age approached, Whittier relied more on his growing mystical awareness of God's actual presence in all men and less on the laws of the Bible and church revelation. The intellectual content and moral insight contained in Whittier's poems are not original nor striking; but unpretentious and well-used as the verses he expressed them in, these thoughts do manifest a grasp of the problems, aspirations, and needs of the common man.

ఇ§ ફ≈

Paradoxically, the once eagerly awaited poetic acclaim now came unsought and unexpectedly as Whittier returned to poetry in the 1850's. Unaware of how well he was reflecting the public's weariness with sectional dispute, Whittier wrote of the innocent boyhood days on the farm, of his lost idealized loves, of gentle Merrimack scenes, of famous Essex County personages, and of local superstitions. A reading public, surprised at this milder side of the militant Quaker, eagerly responded. After the founding of the *Atlantic Monthly* in 1857 Whittier reached a wider audience and for the first time in his life enjoyed comparative financial security.

Nevertheless, when the war came Whittier's fierce loyalty to the Union overcame his Quaker pacifism and expressed itself in two of the most famous poems of the war. "Ein feste Burg ist unser Gott," published in 1861, lashes out against the moral corruption of slavery, and from its magnificent opening of "We wait beneath the furnace-blast" to its thundering climax, the poem throbs with Whittier's burning determination to crush slavery's defenders:

> What gives the wheat-field blades of steel?
> What points the rebel cannon?
> What sets the roaring rabble's heel
> On the old star-spangled pennon?
> What breaks the oath
> Of the men o' the South?
> What whets the knife
> For the Union's life?—
> Hark to the answer: Slavery!

After the first battle of Bull Run the hymn was sung by the famed Hutchinson singers to the troops in camp. Its violent antislavery temper caused a commotion and the hymn was barred from all Union camps. Eventually Mr. Hutchinson had Lincoln review the case and after reading the hymn Lincoln remarked that these were "just the songs he wanted his soldiers to hear." Besides "The Battle Hymn of the Republic" and Whitman's tributes to Lincoln, no other war poem was so truly the product of an hour as "Barbara Frietchie" which was born out of a people's need to have its love of country passionately reaffirmed. Though later found to be inaccurate and mercilessly parodied by critics, it enshrined Whittier in the hearts of millions.

When peace came, a war-weary people turned to the bitter task of rebuilding, subconsciously realizing that the past could never be regained. So Whittier's evocation of the simple farm background and of a domestic integrity fast being lost in the crush of industry and business captured a responsive public and made "Snow-Bound" a best seller in 1866. When "The Tent on the Beach" appeared the next year, its success led Whittier to comment: "Think of bagging in this 'tent' of ours an unsuspecting public at the rate of a thousand a day! This will never do. The swindle is awful. Barnum is a saint to us." This late flowering continued unabated and vigorous past his seventieth year. Home-brewed and seasoned with Yankee skill, poems such as "Among the Hills," "The Pressed Gentian," "At Last," "The Sisters," and "The Pennsylvania Pilgrim" still rank among his best.

The themes of peace, love, and serene acceptance of God's will pervade these later poems. The tumultuous problems of Reconstruction, of swift westward expansion, and of developing industrial power found no such emotional response in the poet as had contemporary events of pre-Civil War days. Far removed from the actual reform struggle and even critical of "the humbug of reform," Whittier had only mild interests in strike issues, woman suffrage, and corruption in government. His romantic ballads and genre pieces repeated his earlier successes with local personages and legendary material. Often these late poems echo Longfellow's sentimental manner with their reliance on foreign sources and idealized narrative; and even ballads dealing with authentic native material, such as "The Bay of Seven Islands" and "In the Old South," are diffused with a soft, mellow romanticism and polished diction that mar their realism. But occasionally, he flawlessly captured a rural scene or local personage, as in "Birchbrook Mill" or "Abram Morrison," to render its homespun values simply and directly. His religious poems of future immortality, love of God, and trust in God's mercy reflect the serenity and assurance of his faith. He once wrote: "After all, there is no great use in arguing the question of immortality. One must feel its truth. You cannot climb into heaven on a syllogism." His religious poetry became a universal affirmation of the existence and the power of God for all men.

◄§ §►

Whittier's popularity in the late nineteenth century surpassed even that of Longfellow, for his later years were a series of uninterrupted literary and personal triumphs. The popular image of the fiery reformer hammering out incendiary verses softened to the revered portrait of a white-bearded old man gently spinning out rustic tales of long ago. As George Arms points out in his introduction to *The Fields Were Green,* American popular taste was spoon-fed on an acceptable diet of "decent" democratic themes which stressed optimism, progress, and virtue. These themes were presented in the best "Psalm of Life" manner which demanded no precision of language and no repression of sentimentality or tears. Oliver Wendell Holmes was only reflecting his age's taste when he wrote to Whittier: "I never rise from any of your poems without feeling the refreshment of their free and sweet atmosphere. . . . the morning air of a soul that breathes freely, and always the fragrance of a loving spirit." Under such conditions of religious security, glorification of virtue, and public pride in the abolition of slavery, Whittier became a hallowed American monument and his birthdays were national holidays. One of the most famous celebrations was the *Atlantic Monthly* dinner given for Whittier's seventieth birthday. For once the publicity-shy Quaker was persuaded to receive the acclaim of America's literary patriarchs, Emerson, Longfellow, Holmes, Lowell, and of the new writers, Howells and Twain. Now Whittier was, like the other New England poets, an object of veneration and awe in a class with Mount Vernon and the American flag.

As the years lengthened Whittier found relaxation and comfort with a restricted group of friends and relatives who sheltered him from an inquiring world. The death of his sister Elizabeth in 1864 was a shock for Whittier. As he wrote to a friend: "Notwithstanding her great weakness, I find I was not prepared for the event. It is terrible—the great motive of life seems lost." Elizabeth's wit and vibrancy had protected Whittier from the social demands of fame; her understanding had bulwarked him during the early days of Abolition; and her sympathy and devotion had consoled him in the midst of literary doubts and ill-health. A young niece, appropriately named Elizabeth, assumed these duties for the next ten years, while literary friends in Boston such as the Claflins and Fields opened their homes to Whittier. Also a host of minor woman writers, Lucy Larcom, Gail Hamilton, Celia Thaxter, Sarah Orne Jewett, and others, thrilled by Whittier's interest in their writing and femininely responsive to his long bachelorhood, became frequent visitors. Newspapers continually manufactured romances and engagements for Whittier, but he remained single and able to poke fun at the whole situation in some doggerel:

> Ah, ladies! you love to levy a tax
> On my poor little paper-parcel of fame,
> Yet strange it seems that among you all
> No one was willing to take my name,
> To write and re-write, till the angels pity her,
> The weariful words,
> > Thine truly,
> > > Whittier.

But despite the attentions of close friends, Whittier's final years were lonely. Writing to Oliver Wendell Holmes, Whittier remarked, "We are stranded mariners, the survivors of a lost crew, warming ourselves at a fire kindled from the wreck of our vessel." His humor and tolerance saved him from the worst of isolated old age, but the crowd of interviewers, autograph seekers, and aspiring writers who descended on Amesbury as "pilgrims" going to Mecca exasperated even the patient Whittier. He invented all sorts of stratagems to escape them, but as he ruefully remarked he could lose a "him" but never a "her." A fund of intimate stories and anecdotes from these years reveal Whittier's Yankee wit and his common sense approach to problems. Even the most profound topics of immortality and Quaker worship were humorously treated. Among Whittier's Amesbury neighbors were an old couple who continued to work assiduously so that they might be able to pay their funeral expenses. Upon hearing this, Whittier dryly commented, "Did thee ever know anyone to stick by the way for want of funds?"

With the marriage of his niece in 1876 Whittier vacated his Amesbury home to spend the spring and autumn months with relatives at a secluded, beautifully landscaped, estate in Danvers which he named Oak Knoll. Severe winters were passed with his Cartland relatives in Newburyport, while the New Hampshire coast and inland mountains drew him in the summer. Whittier remained alert and active throughout the 1880's: he published numerous volumes of new verse, received what he called a "nickname" from Harvard—an LL.D., edited the definitive collection of his prose and poetry, and had his last volume, *At Sundown,* privately printed in 1890. On Dec. 17, 1891 Whittier was eighty-four years old. Shortly afterwards he had an almost fatal attack of grippe, but his health improved in the spring and by summertime he was strong enough to visit with friends in Hampton Falls, New Hampshire, near the coast which he loved so well. He took excursions around the countryside and even wrote two poems in honor of Oliver Wendell Holmes. However, on September 3 he suffered a severe paralytic stroke and died on September 7, 1892.

Whittier's death left him seemingly enshrined as one of America's great poets. Less than fifty years completely reversed that opinion. The twentieth century's complete rejection of the genteel tradition and its critical assumption that these writers produced nothing of lasting value need re-examination. In order to justly estimate his achievement a scrutiny of Whittier's poetic theory and practice is now due.

5

~§ POETIC CREED AND PRACTICE

ONLY BY emphasizing the main evolution in Whittier's life and work can one understand his artistic development and critical beliefs. As Harry Hayden Clark has indicated, until 1833 Whittier was primarily a sectional romanticist, a journalistic poet nourished on the strange literary diet of Byron, Burns, and the Bible. His work was blatantly derivative, though his attempts to versify native legends indicated his future capability. A brief political phase as well as hopes for lyric fame were ended when Whittier joined the Abolition party. Whittier's second main phase, from 1833 to the 1850's, was a period of reform and humanitarian interests when he believed law and social action would eradicate evil. The intensity and sincerity of his reform writings purged him of his former self-centeredness and sentimentality. Gradually as the Abolitionists merged with major political parties, Whittier returned to the familiar ground of native legend and boyhood reminiscence. At the same time a deepening religious faith and the terrible effects of sectional dispute lessened his confidence in outward social reform. By 1860 the poet again dominated as Whittier entered his third phase of what has been called his "religious humanism." Now his humanitarian interests were concerned with individualistic striving for moral perfection and he turned to God's mercy, not law, for guidance. Finally, the long pent-up memories of his farm background and lost dreams provided inspiration for his best poetry.

≈§ §≈

Whittier's mature views on art and beauty reflect the early conflict between the lure of external natural beauty and the strict plainness of his Quaker training. From earliest childhood Whittier was rigorously disciplined to hold that sensuous beauty and the fine arts lure men away from spiritual goodness. The Quaker attitude toward the arts was negative—do not read novels, do not attend the theatre, do not listen to music—all of which was based on a belief that human impulses are divorced from the Divine. Like the early Puritans the Quakers feared that a delight in external sensuous beauty would replace inner spiritual perfection. So Whittier's earliest verses stress a beauty of holiness and sanctity. Yet his imitation of Byron and Willis indicates the growing struggle between his religious training and his ardent emotional spirit. In an early fictional attempt he has an opium eater rhapsodize on the witchery of his former love: "It is idle to talk of the superior attraction of intellectual beauty, when compared with mere external loveliness . . . the beauty of form and color, the grace of motion, the harmony of tone, are seen and felt and appreciated at once." Of course this imitates prevailing literary modes and only imaginatively mirrors the young Quaker's personal views on beauty; yet it does highlight part of the emotional turmoil undoubtedly taking place in his own mind. Though he avowedly condemned the sensuous, it intrigued him. Similarly his early statements on art emphasize its supernatural mission and the godlike creativeness of the artist. For a time he believed that the art of poetry could be an end in itself, rising above the moral issues of life, existing in its own domain of fancy and imagination. He wrote glowing tributes to Chatterton and Byron, echoing their desire for one "high and haughty hour . . . One grasp at fleeting power."

However, in 1833 the remains of these romantic dreams were swept completely away when Whittier joined the Abolitionist movement. Its moral and humanitarian bases strengthened Whittier's Quaker belief in the equality of man and the evil of slavery, and the cause widened his purely personal goal of poetic fame into a universal desire to write for all humanity. So the "dreamer

47

born" whose "eye was beauty's powerless slave" found a sterner guide than soft romance. "The Reformer," a poem typical of Whittier's feelings during the next twenty years, shows how far this passionate devotion carried him. The reformer is the "strong one" who destroys the godless shrines of church, wealth, custom, and power to build a new world from the ruins of the old. Significantly, he demolishes monuments of art and beauty, ignoring the sad surprise of "young romance." Naive as the poem's belief in the efficacy of outward reform may be, its fervid moralistic tone echoes Whittier's feelings at this time. Now his poems emphasized the beauty of ethical action and repudiated the romantic concept of the poet's imaginative power. In a characteristic literary criticism he remarked of Longfellow's "A Psalm of Life": "These nine simple verses are worth more than all the dreams of Shelley, and Keats, and Wordsworth. They are alive and vigorous with the spirit of the day in which we live—the moral steam enginery of an age of action." Art per se became anathema as the rigid demands of this moral warfare refined his Quaker asceticism and strengthened his sentimental lyricism. Yet despite these unimaginative and stifling tenets Whittier still wrote ballads and genre pieces which minimized moral content. His Abolitionist conscience had to justify even these and so he excused his romantic "Amy Wentworth" by saying that the soft play of art has its function in providing temporary relief from the tensions of moral reform. Art viewed as an escape from editorial pressures and political action was far removed from his earlier desire to immortalize it as a source of pure unfading joy. After the Civil War Whittier tempered his austere denunciation of nonmoralistic art and admitted that it beguiled his lonely hours and refreshed his memories of the past, but it still seemed of secondary value and questionable worth.

Whittier's fullest statement on the function of art came in "The Tent on the Beach" (1867). Here he presented his final view, a minor reconciliation between the doctrine of art for art's sake and an art which only serves moral ends. He admits that his poetry has been too moralistic and that his ethical conscience has thwarted fancy's imaginative flight. However, when one of the speakers in the poem comments that art needs no other justification than beauty itself, Whittier responds characteristically:

> Better so [i.e., to have a moral in poetry]
> Than bolder flights that know no check;
> Better to use the bit, than throw
>   The reins all loose on fancy's neck.
> The liberal range of Art should be
> The breadth of Christian liberty.

Whittier concludes by saying that the truth of art, its faithfulness to the dicta of Christianity, does not need the "garnish of a lie," and that elements of beauty for their own sake are not necessary for good poetry. Confusing religion with aesthetics, Whittier's concept of the function of art remained obscured throughout his life.

Of course Whittier's intense reform activity strengthened his devotion to literature based on Christian goodness and truth, and this conviction formed an essential part of his mature views on beauty. Once his reform interests lessened, his confidence in outward action and social progress changed to a reliance on inner values and individual quest; and his concept of the beautiful and its relationship to the artist deepened accordingly. The beauty of silence and peace, fundamental to his belief in the Quaker doctrine of the Inner Light, assumed a larger and more influential role in his poetry. Perhaps the best expression of his changing views is an essay entitled "The Beautiful." This article fully indicates the transition Whittier was making from his stringent Abolitionist position to a more inclusive view of beauty. It states unequivocally that the external elements of form and shape do not constitute the beautiful. Rather, true beauty arises from the mind as a radiation of "holiness, of purity, of that inward grace that passeth show." The artist must discern in the "outward environment . . . a deeper and more real loveliness," an inner spiritual beauty which transcends rules and techniques.

Obviously this idea of beauty is intimately connected with his belief in the Inner Light, which maintained that the indwelling of the Holy Spirit in each man is a personal, introspective experience, and, at times, a mystical relationship. In striving for individual perfection, no set dogma or creed is followed, only the subjective voice of the Inner Light. So when Whittier commented that "Beauty, in and of itself, is good" he meant something far different from Keats's similar statement. Following Emerson's

49

organic view of art, Whittier believed that goodness, truth, and beauty were one and that the material was only a reflection of the divine archetype. As a corollary, Whittier held that the appreciation of beauty was a personal thing which could be achieved anywhere and by anyone. The attraction of an external object was dependent on "an instantaneous reflection as to its history, purpose, or associations." Such a view followed the prevailing Romantic belief in the subjectivity of the beautiful—that the mind not only received but also created in its appreciation of the beautiful. Thus, beauty was no longer intrinsic or absolute in the Neoclassic sense but dependent upon states of mind, resulting from associations enkindled in our imaginations by external objects. Whittier's mature application of this doctrine was far removed from his earlier fascination with Byron's insights into forbidden vice and the Romantics' fondness for psychological subtleties and sensuous experience. Now his interests centered on quiet admiration for the common beauty of daily life which would elevate and inspire readers rather than thrill or tantalize them.

One other aspect of the doctrine of associations, its connection of the material and spiritual worlds, is investigated by Whittier in an article, "Swedenborg." Whittier lauds the power of Swedenborg's transcendental theories in stripping bare the sense objects of the world to reveal "the types and symbols of the world of spirit." Stressing the associations that an imaginative man like Swedenborg could make between the "facts" of this world and the spiritual values of the next, Whittier also praises his realistic expression of these abstract ideas. This relation of the spiritual to the material and the importance of personal associations upheld in a theoretical way the practical, religious training of Quakerism and further strengthened Whittier's moral view of beauty. More importantly it led him to perceive that an accurate record of his personal experiences could reveal the implicit values hidden beneath the physical form. So, tardily, Whittier found in the ordinary things of life—his farm background, the local Haverhill scenery, his knowledge of Quaker history, the Essex County legends, his boyhood memories—factual images that could be transmuted by personal associations and imaginative effort into authentic, worthwhile materials for poetry. The romance that he hoped to find in these familiar things was based on the awareness that humble experiences and simple feelings had as much wonder and beauty as his former dreams "of lands of gold and pearl,/Of loving knight and lady." This theory of the beauty of the commonplace formed the cornerstone for his finest poems written in the 1850's. Now his subject matter, such as an old rhyme about a calloused Marblehead skipper, his birthplace in a snowstorm, a girl raking hay on a summer's day, or a local tale about a Hampton witch, was based directly on the commonplace incidents of his own experience.

Associated with this final understanding of the proper material for his writing was the problem of finding the appropriate manner for expressing these feelings. From his earlier literary experiments he came to believe that style was the communication of an emotion or an idea in the clearest, most direct manner. He especially appreciated books which were written from an inner spiritual prompting and which dressed truth in a somber guise, rather than garnishing it by elaborate stylistic devices. This truth of style actually meant a fidelity to personal experience, a realization of one's own powers and insights, and an attempt to present them in the clearest possible manner. Belatedly Whittier understood the important relationship between the emotional experiences of a man and his method of expression. In theory, at least, Whittier was presenting the organic belief that form should follow function. When joined to his love of the commonplace, this truth of style enabled Whittier to see the harm of surface ornamentation and rhetorical tricks. He believed that a writer must be himself first and then establish his style; that the inner emotional quality of a work soars above mere literary technique; and finally, that the subject matter must bear a direct relationship to the author's own personal experiences. Though this emphasis on truth often caused Whittier to overmoralize, it never allowed him to equate sincerity with dullness.

৺৪ ৯৶

Of course theory is one thing, while practice is another. Whittier had more than the usual difficulty in properly organizing his material and his mature method of composition reflects his early formative influences. Most noticeable is the didactic bent of certain recurring themes. The value of domestic emotions, the rewards of true love, the innocence of childhood, the necessity of social equality, and the nobility of ethical action repeat the stock ideas of the nineteenth century. In presenting these moral lessons Whittier often took the nucleus of the story from another source —an old legend, an account from history, or even a contemporary event. This was recast in a realistic narrative with a concluding discussion of the moral application of the tale. This technique is found in such widely divergent ventures as the nature poem, "The Vanishers," where an Indian legend of the dead returning for their loved ones leads to the consolation that all the losses will be reclaimed in heaven; the ballad, "The Garrison of Cape Ann," where the Colonial legend of spectre warriors teaches the value of prayer; and the philosophic "Miriam," where the Oriental concepts of God affirm the universality of truth as Miriam uses Christian doctrine to quell the rage of a heathen king. The tagged-on moral is a serious aesthetic failing which plagued Whittier throughout his life. In his best poems, however, such as "Skipper Ireson's Ride" or "The Trailing Arbutus," the lesson achieves an organic harmony and artistically develops the implications of the narrative.

Unfortunately this excessive moralizing is often joined to a melodramatic situation which is diffusely presented and senti-mentally resolved. Whittier never fully eradicated Gothic over-tones from his work and the years of hastily written reform verse conditioned him to the ease of stock phrases and wordy generalizations. "The Swan Song of Parson Avery" shows a mature Whittier depending on these hackneyed devices. The tragedy of the shipwrecked parson is presented by commonplace, flat terms and a stereotyped listing, "wild waves and the blast," "woman's wail and man's despair." The climax reveals Avery as the only survivor clinging to a rock, praying:

> In the baptism of these waters wash white my every sin,
> And let me follow up to Thee my household and my kin!
> Open the sea-gate of Thy heaven, and let me enter in!

The improbability of the scene is heightened by Parson Avery's rhetoric and the use of ludicrous images like "sea-gate" and "baptism." Also, the awkwardly phrased ending picture of the angels leaning over walls of crystal to hear Avery's hymn ("as the strong wave swept him downward the sweet hymn upward pressed") destroys all dramatic effect. Unhappily for Whittier's art, the public thrived upon such melodrama and he responded to their taste. Still Whittier could succeed with melodrama. The situation in "Barbara Frietchie" is excessively theatrical as an old woman defies a Confederate band and brings a blush of shame to Stonewall Jackson's face; but Whittier's presentation saves it. The bare diction, the concreteness and simplicity of the rural setting, and the artistic use of ballad rhythm and folk imagery give the poem an effective dramatic tone.

Whittier's mastery of local color techniques, his painter-like ability to describe accurately the native scene, characterizes his finest poems. In them the natural scene remains unchanged, for Whittier transcribed rather than created and represented rather than arranged. The artistic value of this approach depended on the skill and selectivity of his recording. The following lines from "The Countess" are a close literal picture of Rocks Village on the Merrimack River:

> Over the wooded northern ridge,
>   Between its houses brown,
> To the dark tunnel of the bridge
>   The street comes straggling down.
>
> .   .   .   .
>
> With salt sea-scents along its shores
>   The heavy hay-boats crawl,
> The long antennae of their oars
>   In lazy rise and fall.

Yet its salient characteristics are exaggerated and heightened to create an atmosphere of drowsiness and the "stranded" quality of a bypassed town. Closely connected with the pictorial cast of his mind is Whittier's use of decorative and pictorial imagery. Usually associated with his rural background, these images evoke a mild sense response lacking the richness and complexity of the expansive imagery used by Walt Whitman and Emily Dickinson. The visual presentation of his ideas draws heavily on common farm imagery—planting, growth of crops, harvesting, husking, change of seasons—and biblical analogues. So an old teacher's antiquarian interests are described as "threshing time's neglected sheaves" and a girl's mind is seen as "dew-moist and bright . . . Unfolding like a morning flower." Whittier particularly delighted in detailed listings, an accumulation of picturesque images selected for an overall tone. In "Among the Hills" the first twenty lines sensuously evoke the languid quiet of a sultry summer's day. The enervating heat of the sun becomes a palpable object which oppresses flowers, tires the wind, and mesmerizes animals and human beings. The skillful association of these objects imaginatively creates a "pervading symphony of peace."

Following his "truth of style" concept and use of local color effects, Whittier did attempt to simplify his expression and to employ the language of the common man. Often hackneyed phrasings and overused images exploit this aspect all too well. Whittier wrote far too much and when inspiration lagged he fell back on stock phrases and previously used images. A repetitious light–dark comparison mars many of his religious poems as does a chain–fetters image in his Abolitionist poetry. His notoriously bad rhymes also fit this pattern. The moralizing couplet in "Maud Muller" is the most famous example:

> For of all sad words of tongue or pen,
> The saddest are these: "It might have been!"

Yet even here Whittier is preserving a regional tendency to blur the distinction between "i" and "e" sounds. Many of his apparently false rhymes are in perfect accord with local New England pronunciation. His rhyming of "Susquehanna" with "banner" was and is New England practice. Some of his combinations such as "haunt" and "chant" are archaic, but others are suspended rhymes like the bold pairings found in Emily Dickinson's poems. Whittier understood the regional quality of his rhymes and so was unconcerned when his rough associations jarred the cultured ears of Lowell. This lack of interest in matters of form is no excuse for his undeniably poor rhymes, careless diction, and grammatical blunders; but often these "Yankeeisms" preserve the folk flavor of his verse and add to its authenticity.

Another outstanding characteristic of Whittier's style is the Neoclassic bent of his versification, diction, and imagery. Though maturing in an age of Romantic experimentation with verse and meter, Whittier retained an almost Colonial approach to form. His poems use the simplest of meters, the ballad and octosyllabic, while the eighteenth century's rhyming couplet and alternate rhyme are his usual stanzaic form. Rhetorical balance and set parallelisms, such as appear in "The Barefoot Boy," dated his poems even in his own day:

> How the robin feeds her young,
> How the oriole's nest is hung;
> Where the whitest lilies blow,
> Where the freshest berries grow,
> Where the ground-nut trails its vine,
> Where the wood-grape's clusters shine.

Similar devices which made his art somewhat old-fashioned are his pairing of adjectives and his characteristic inversions, which tend to create slow, halting rhythm as in these lines from "Cassandra Southwick":

> And there were ancient citizens, cloak-wrapped and grave and cold,
> And grim and stout sea-captains with faces bronzed and old,
> And on his horse with Rawson, his cruel clerk at hand,
> Sat dark and haughty Endicott, the ruler of the land.

In his imagery there is a preponderance of set comparisons and a fondness for personifications in the Neoclassic manner. Similarly his ending comments on the application of the poem are often introduced by "so" or "like." For smoothness and sound effects Whittier repeatedly used standard alliterative devices with assonance and onomatopoeia. All of these techniques were the well-worn ones of the previous century.

However, a fuller examination of his poetry indicates that these technical inadequacies do not always detract from his artistic achievement. Whittier's realistic genre pieces show his art at its best, as a natural and an intimate part of his own experience. In these pieces Whittier succeeds, for in them he is, as he once said of Robert Dinsmore, "part and parcel of the rural life of New England,—one who had grown strong amidst its healthful influences, familiar with all its details, and capable of detecting whatever of beauty, humor, or pathos pertain to it,—one who has added to his book-lore the large experience of an active participation in the rugged toil, the hearty amusements, the trials, and the pleasures of the life he describes." Whittier's regional poems firmly heed the essential truth that he had first recognized in Burns's poems—that within the most commonplace objects lie rich poetic materials. These poems convey his inner love for the environment that molded him and the traditions that inspired him, and reveal his extensive knowledge of local scenery, custom, and history. Here his style, as he theoretically wished it to be, is sincere and direct, purged of its glaring rhetorical and sentimental flaws; the descriptions are graphic and picturesque; and the materials of home, nature, and affections are fashioned into enduring poetry.

⋖§ §⋗

How successfully Whittier could apply his beliefs to poetry may be seen by an examination of "Telling the Bees." The story hinges on a local Essex County superstition that a death in the family would drive away the bees and that the custom of draping the hives in black mourning colors would prevent this. The narrative itself records the delayed visit of a young man to the farm-house of his beloved Mary. The tone of the poem is informal, almost conversational, and Whittier relates the tale as if he and the reader were rewalking the ground on which it took place. In the first lines, directly addressing this reader and insisting that he follow the scene closely, Whittier points out:

> Here is the place; right over the hill
> Runs the path I took;
> You can see the gap in the old wall still,
> And the stepping-stones in the shallow brook.
>
> There is the house, with the gate red-barred
> And the poplars tall;
> And the barn's brown length, and the cattle-yard
> And the white horns tossing above the wall.

The details are plain and unelaborated: the poplars are merely "tall," the barn just "brown," and the cattle are depicted only by "white horns." The series of "ands" connect one detail to the next in almost childlike fashion. Then, as if pausing in this trip with the reader, the poet notes that, although a year has passed, everything is still the same:

> And the same rose blows, and the same sun glows,
> And the same brook sings of a year ago.

This emphasis on external "sameness" is the unifying element of the three occasions involved in the story: the young man's earliest visit to Mary; then the eager call a month later which he is reconstructing for the reader; and now his return with the reader, after a year, to the scene of that visit; on each occasion the scene has appeared almost unchanged. Thus, the poet recalls how care-fully he had prepared for his reunion with Mary a year ago; then, reliving that past moment he excitedly exclaims, "I can see it all now . . . just the same as a month before,—" and repeats the description of the opening stanzas, uniting the scene of both past visits with that of the present.

But the mood changes when the poet recalls, though almost casually, that coming closer to the house he noticed "nothing changed but the hives of bees." For this one small detail breaks the continuity and with increasing tension we hear with him again the drearily singing chore girl and see the ominous shreds of black on the hives. The warm June sun of the moment before now chills like snow as the eventual discovery is foreshadowed. Still, the boy refuses to abandon his former confidence and as-sumes that Mary's grandfather must be dead. But then he sees the old man sitting on the porch, "and the chore-girl still/Sung to the bees." Finally he is close enough to understand the song of the chore girl:

> "Stay at home, pretty bees, fly not hence!
> Mistress Mary is dead and gone!"

With effective absence of comment, Whittier concludes the poem with this revelation of Mary's death and allows the reader to supply the resulting horror and impact of the loss.

Only then is the reader aware of the skillful manipulation of theme, as the careful development of the attractiveness and as-surance of external nature hides the inevitable destruction of human beauty and earthly love. The ironic contrast of the boy's trust and expectation with the true situation offers a psychological insight into the problem of death and man's inability to prepare for its shocking occurrence. As a whole the poem succeeds because of the utter simplicity of its proselike diction and ballad meter, and because of its firm structural unity created by the progression from assurance to fear and then surprise. The stylistic devices are few: some repetitions in the use of the adjective "same" and similar physical detail; some parallelisms, such as the balance in "heave and slow," "forward and back"; some alliteration as in the "s" sounds of the last stanzas; and a restatement of detail with a changed significance when the warm sun is transformed into the chilling snow and the happy song of the brook is altered into the dreary chant of death. Yet the poem's seeming artlessness shows Whittier's mastery of simple narration, his truth of style, while its theme employs a rural situation and local environment to emphasize an underlying pathos in human existence. Like the best of Whittier's other genre pieces and ballads, this poem demonstrates the validity of his mature application of the beauty of the commonplace.

6

_{๕ड} THE BALLADS

E XCLUDING his genre poems, Whittier's ballads probably represent his finest poetic achievement and the best re-creation of native folklore and legend written in the nineteenth century. His ballads, especially, express his lifelong interest in New England history and wide knowledge of local customs and superstitions. Still the formation of these ballads was a tortuous process which reveals how slowly Whittier's artistry matured and how tardily he recognized his own abilities. Only when dealing with material that was intimately associated with his Quaker beliefs, rural background, humanitarian interests, and Essex region could Whittier produce poetry of artistic quality and enduring merit.

In general Whittier's ballads remain remarkably true to the characteristics of traditional folk balladry. Like Sir Walter Scott, Whittier was genuinely responsive to the spirit of folk narrative, having the background knowledge necessary to embody popular feeling and legend in narrative song. His best ballads are realistic and direct, centralizing on dramatic action and developing one main theme. As in traditional ballads the tragic overtones of the theme evolve from the basic emotions of love, hate, loyalty, and betrayal with particular emphasis on an individual rebellion against society. Whittier's diction is usually sparse and simple, while his images are commonplace and filled with folk expression.

Even so, lyric and pastoral effects often hinder dramatic action and mar the objectivity so necessary for good balladry. Nor do the ballads escape his habitual "moral squint."

Though many American poets wrote ballads in the nineteenth century, only Whittier and Longfellow attempted to narrate folk and native material in a large number of their verses. Most of Longfellow's ballads utilize European folk tales or chivalric romances to glorify the past and create an atmosphere of melancholy. Some of them, such as his longer narratives "Evangeline" and "The Song of Hiawatha," do employ native material and are polished attempts to create beauty and romance in the American scene. His most famous ballad, "The Wreck of the Hesperus," dramatizes a moment of action that is purely American, the wreck of a schooner near Gloucester in 1839, or actually the wrecks of several ships there during a severe storm. The form is faultless, the story's movement is light and smooth, and the idiom remains simple. The structure is good, building to the disaster with the warning of the old sailor and its scornful dismissal by the confident captain. However, the storm and the captain's fears for his daughter are melodramatically and sentimentally presented. Also noticeable is the lack of realistic setting and definite locale, for Longfellow does little more than refer to the "reef of Norman's woe." In contrast is Whittier's ballad "The Wreck of Rivermouth," which also suffers from an excess of melodrama and moralizing, but in Whittier's poem the unreality of the actual situation is bulwarked by a realistic account of the storm and the story is inseparably tied to the New England coastline by a concrete description of the locale.

Most of Longfellow's ballads are far from the spirit of traditional ones. Their conscious poetic devices and sentimental handling of narrative destroy drama, while the subjects used have little relation to his own experience. The dream world of the past when culled from foreign sources is hardly conducive to the production of typical American ballads. It is precisely on this point of realism and local atmosphere that Whittier displays superiority to Longfellow, for he produced ballads which typified the American heritage and expressed its values. Whittier lived his life in the main currents of his age as editor, Abolitionist, and politician; he knew and loved his generation; and by background, religious training, and study he could sympathize with the previous ones. As a Quaker, Whittier's earliest readings and instructions had been from the journals and histories of the Friends, which contained accounts of the persecutions endured by the original Quaker settlers. Whittier grew up revering Quakers such as Margaret Brewster and Samuel Shattuck who suffered for their beliefs, and admiring those who resisted intolerance such as Thomas Macy and Cassandra Southwick, while his later researches into Colonial history gave him a sympathetic insight into the nature of the Puritan theocracy and the reasons for the persecutions. Then his isolated rural upbringing made him completely dependent on his family and the surrounding district for intellectual growth and emotional maturity, and the close ties formed by years of permanent association with one place instilled in him a love of locality and all the traditions connected with it. His imaginative, responsive mind never forgot the tales told around the Whittier fireplace about Essex County witches, popular superstitions, or local personages such as Floyd Ireson and Mary Ingalls. It was from these sources that Whittier obtained the material for some of his best ballads.

◆§ §◆

Fortunately for Whittier, his earliest literary influences were the poems of Burns, which glorified rural life and local customs, and the romances of Scott, which centered on the heroism of Scottish warriors. His imitations of these two men, or at least his use of their themes as he saw them reflected in his own life, were the most promising verses of his early years. His first collection of poems and tales, *Legends of New England*, dealt entirely with local traditions and superstitions. The verses are marred by digressions and extravagant romantic phrasing and employ the typical Gothic devices of doomed lovers, ghostly ships, and hidden horrors. However, one ballad, "The Black Fox," has a sure poetic beat and adapts its subject and content to the ballad tradition of simplicity. The introduction to the poem recreates the atmosphere of a winter's evening in rural New England with a clearness of language and simplicity of diction that indicate Whittier's ballad capabilities. The grandmother is an excellent choice as narrator with her homespun descriptions and superstitious nature, while her account of the mysterious activities of the black fox effectively conveys a rural delight in the supernatural. Though the story is artificial, even sentimental in parts, it minimizes Gothic horror and eliminates moralizing—a marked advance over Whittier's other ballad attempts.

Another early ballad is "The Song of the Vermonters" (1833). Its theme, a rallying cry for all patriotic Vermonters to defend their state during the Revolutionary War, is an obvious imitation of Scott's border romances; its form, rhyming couplets with a basic anapestic beat, gives a martial ring to the whole:

> Ho—all to the borders! Vermonters, come down,
> With your breeches of deerskin and jackets of brown;
> With your red woolen caps, and your moccasins, come,
> To the gathering summons of trumpet and drum.

The poem's local color descriptions of the countryside, boastful praise of Vermont's qualities, and defiant challenge to "all the world" are conscious attempts to present the song as an authentic ballad. In fact, Whittier predated the poem 1779. Despite its rhetorical air, characteristic moralizing, and poetic language, many sections do accord with good ballad presentation. This poem indicates how close Whittier was to having the right medium for expressing his deep-rooted feelings about the New England past.

During the next fifteen years, Whittier only intermittently followed the path marked out by these pioneer pieces, as his Abolitionist work demanded his full attention. Still, some of his antislavery poems show the experiments that he was making with ballad technique. "The Hunters of Men" (1835) is a caustic satire on the newest southern amusement, the tracking down of escaped slaves. Opening his poem in the best chivalric manner, Whittier establishes the atmosphere of a medieval chase with his invitation for all to come hunting:

> Have ye heard of our hunting, o'er mountain and glen,
> Through cane-brake and forest—the hunting of men?
> The lords of our land to this hunting have gone,
> As the fox-hunter follows the sound of the horn;
> Hark! the cheer and hallo! the crack of the whip.

The archaic words, the courtly adjectives, and the titling of the hunters as "lords" are all devices of olden romances; while the use of a refrain, "the hunting of men," and the conscious repe-

Whittier about 1870, Photograph

titions of similar phrases and sound patterns are part of established ballad technique. These gracious phrases and romantic images are ironically contrasted with the inhuman purpose of the hunt—the killing of men. With heavy-handed satire Whittier continues this romantic pretense crying out: "Gay luck to our hunters" and "Oh, goodly and grand is our hunting to see." The irony fails when Whittier depicts priests, politicians, mothers, and daughters merrily hunting the slaves; he had not yet learned the restraint and understatement necessary for finished satiric art and true ballad creation.

⚜

One of his first real ballads is "The Exiles," written in 1841. It shows how a decade of Abolitionist work had matured him, and, conversely, how far he had yet to go for poetic maturity. Certainly his antislavery writing had enlarged his sense of the dramatic, developed his awareness of emotional appeal, and taught him the necessity of direct statement. The plot of "The Exiles" is aptly suited to ballad demands for an exciting, realistic narrative, since it is the tale of Thomas Macy's flight down the Merrimack River to escape persecution for harboring a Quaker. Its theme, the dramatic struggle of one man against existing injustice, stresses the value of inner principle over outward law. Everything was within the range of Whittier's talents and interests, for he had grown up in the Merrimack Valley and had spent the greater part of his life fighting for freedom and resisting intolerance. Yet he failed to develop the poem artistically. It is overly long (sixty stanzas) and greatly weakened by numerous digressions and pious interjections, while its labored comparisons and sentimental tone ignore the realism of good balladry. Over half the poem deals with a wordy description of the fleeing Quaker and his eventual capture—all of which distract from the central drama of Macy's courage and flight.

However, there is a fine ballad meter, and touches in the story demonstrate how naturally Whittier could portray characters and how realistically he could sketch in background settings. The inner serenity of the old Quaker is described as the covering of "autumn's moonlight," while the frustrated priest is seen with his "grave cocked hat" gone and his dishevelled wig hanging behind him "like some owl's nest . . . upon a thorn." The flight

of Macy down the Merrimack is simply presented through selected scenes of nearby communities:

> The fisher wives of Salisbury—
> The men were all away—
> Looked out to see the stranger oar
> Upon their waters play.
>
> Deer Island's rocks and fir-trees threw
> Their sunset-shadows o'er them,
> And Newbury's spire and weathercock
> Peered o'er the pines before them.

❧ ☙

"Cassandra Southwick," written in 1843, shows a considerable
advance over "The Exiles" in dramatic structure and presentation. Here, too, the incident is one culled from the history of
Quaker persecutions; but instead of relating the complete story
behind Cassandra's imprisonment, Whittier concentrates on the
fears and doubts of the girl as she waits to be sold into slavery.
The early section of the poem, though overlong and rhetorical, probes the nature of Cassandra's fears and near despair.
Her simple, trusting spirit is prey to all the distorted visions that
the night and the unknown can bring. Torturedly she contrasts
her past rural childhood, her shy hopes of romance, and her open
delight in nature against her present imprisonment for following
the "crazy fancies" of the Quakers. Fearfully she imagines the
insults and pain that her gentle feminine nature will soon be subject to. Though her language is platitudinous and filled with biblical allusions, it fits her religious spirit and farm background.
Finally prayer and her recollections of other martyrs dispel the
nightmarish terrors. Once dawn breaks, the movement is swift
and dramatic as she is led to the wharves. Whittier pauses briefly
to show her dazed response to the bright sunlight, the idle laugh-
ter of the crowd, and the rough handling by the sheriff. Her
shame under the glare of the curious onlookers and her pathetic
cry for God's aid increase the tenseness of the scene. As she approaches the docks, Whittier conveys the atmosphere of a sea
town with the briefest possible detail:

> We paused at length, where at my feet the sunlit waters broke
> On glaring reach of shining beach, and shingly wall of rock;

65

The merchant-ships lay idly there, in hard clear lines on high,
Tracing with rope and slender spar their network on the sky.

And there were ancient citizens, cloak-wrapped and grave and cold,
And grim and stout sea-captains with faces bronzed and old.

All the characters, including the clerk Rawson and Governor
Endicott, are generalized—only briefly seen by the hesitant
glances of the young girl. Under the taunts of the sheriff, Cassandra defends her innocence, while her passionate outcry and
complete helplessness win the sympathy of the crowd. The cap-
tains remain silent as the sheriff repeatedly calls for a volunteer
to sell Cassandra into slavery. Finally, one answers:

Pile my ship with bars of silver, pack with coins of Spanish gold,
From keel-piece up to deck-plank, the roomage of her hold,
By the living God who made me!—I would sooner in your bay
Sink ship and crew and cargo, than bear this child away!

An aroused crowd now roars its approval and turns on Endicott
and his followers. As they leave, Cassandra is freed; unfortunately
the denouement is prolonged by Cassandra's fervent thanksgiving
to God. Still the nucleus of the story is well told and it does have
a swift dramatic movement. Whittier's use of the first person
narrative gives an immediacy to the action and deepens the tale
by an examination of her mental fears and religious doubts. The
heavy religious imagery and allusions strengthen the underlying
theme—that God protects his own. Throughout, the repetition
of key words, the series of "and" connectives, and the parallelisms
of adjectives and nouns create a definite folk flavor. The descrip-
tive imagery is of the simplest kind: Rawson's cheek is "wine-
empurpled," the captain growls back his answer like "the roaring
of the sea," and Endicott looks at the disapproving crowd with
a "lion glare." Though the poem is overlong and didactic, it is
a long step from the discursive and dramatically weak "The
Exiles." Whittier had found his proper subject matter and was
now approaching surety of presentation.

◅§ ৈ

Another ballad of the same year, "The New Wife and the
Old," deals with a local superstition which Whittier had heard
as a child about the power of dead spirits. Though its consciously

set mood of terror and suspense is somewhat reminiscent of Gothic narrative, its excellent style holds the reader's interest:

> Dark the halls, and cold the feast,
> Gone the bridemaids, gone the priest.
> All is over, all is done.
>
> .   .   .   .
>
> Hushed within and hushed without,
> Dancing feet and wrestlers' shout;
> Dies the bonfire on the hill;
> All is dark and all is still.

The repetitions of similar verb patterns and the balance of phrases with their recurrence in later stanzas establish a mood of waiting and anxiety. The resulting drama does not quite live up to this effective introduction as the young bride has her wedding ring and bracelet melodramatically stolen by the ghost of a former wife. Near the end of the story, interest switches from the terror and wonder of the new bride to an examination of the sinful conscience of the older husband. Also Whittier upsets the unity of the story by musing on the supernatural reasons for the dead wife's action. Still, the ballad technique is sure and the story concentrates on the one main incident without undue moralizing.

ఆక్షి ఫ్రిహ

During the next ten years the pressures of editorial and journalistic duties caused Whittier to write mainly prose; consequently he neglected his ballads. Two ballads of this period merit attention, however, "Barclay of Ury" and "Kathleen." "Barclay of Ury" (1847) expands the general theme of "Cassandra Southwick" in dealing with the indignities heaped upon an old warrior for joining the Quakers. Again the story turns on the conflict of inner conviction versus outward ridicule with the added irony that Barclay's former friends now abuse him, feeling that he betrayed their trust. The simple diction and unadorned tone are in perfect keeping with ballad objectivity and directness, while the religious note is intimately connected with Barclay's character. As he slowly rides through his native town, secure in the strength of the Inner Light, his dignity is contrasted with the emotional outbursts of the surrounding mob. The slow deliberate beat of the verse echoes the measured pace of his horse, indicating his unflinching religious confidence and determination to pursue his Quaker course despite all threats. The climax of the poem occurs when a former comrade rushes to his defense and pleads with Barclay to fight the crowd. His bewilderment when Barclay refuses to fight re-echoes the mob's previous betrayal, while his pity moves Barclay as violence never could. This meeting serves as the dramatic introduction to Barclay's simple testament of faith. He contrasts past glory and acclaim with his present debasement and admits that it is hard to lose friends, to be humiliated, and "to learn forgiving"; but, realizing that "God's own time is best," he can endure all—so he goes his own way, completely alone. Whittier should have ended the ballad with this moving speech which grew organically out of a definite dramatic situation. Instead he tagged on a moral of four stanzas which marred an otherwise fine ballad. Still the portrait of Barclay is Whittier's first successful investigation of those reserved, stiff figures whose utter simplicity and tenacious faith reveal a sense of elemental power.

The other ballad of this period, "Kathleen" (1849), shows Whittier's complete mastery of ballad technique. Purporting to be a tale of old Ireland sung by a wandering Irish scholar, the poem does not have a local theme, but its content and style are handled in traditional ballad manner. The story relates the selling of a beautiful Irish girl to the American colonies by her cruel stepmother, a later rescue by a young lover, and a safe return to her sorrowing father. The first stanzas immediately begin the narrative with the marriage of the "mighty lord" of "Galaway" to another wife; the second stanza marks out the conflict in the ballad, the new wife's favoring of her own child to the neglect of Kathleen. A few stanzas later, Kathleen is introduced and warning is given of her coming doom. In traditional ballad fashion, dialogue is used throughout to convey feeling and action: no motivation is given for the stepmother's sudden decision to sell Kathleen; and there is no plausible explanation for her triumph over the old lord's love for his daughter. The art in these following stanzas is a thing of the utmost simplicity:

> Oh, then spake up the angry dame,
>   "Get up, get up," quoth she,
> "I'll sell ye over Ireland,
>   I'll sell ye o'er the sea!"

> She clipped her glossy hair away,
>   That none her rank might know,
> She took away her gown of silk,
>   And gave her one of tow,
>
> And sent her down to Limerick town
>   And to a seaman sold
> This daughter of an Irish lord
>   For ten good pounds in gold.

This objective tone is preserved throughout and the scholar's final summation, in perfect keeping with his function as a wandering minstrel, provides the desired happy ending. Noticeable too is the absence of sophisticated imagery; only the most conventional descriptions are given: the girl is "fair" and "the flower of Ireland"; her arm is "snowy-white" and her hand "snow-white"; and the stepmother is seen as "angry" and "evil." This ballad readily illustrates the progress Whittier had made from his early uneven, discursive ballads.

❧ ☙

Whittier was now at the height of his poetic powers and the next twenty years were to witness the writing of his best ballads. In 1828 Whittier first heard from a schoolmate at Haverhill Academy the song of Skipper Ireson's being tarred and feathered by the women of Marblehead. It was a typical folk song known to all the inhabitants of the town—perfect material for a poet who knew the locale and understood the mentality of the people. At that time Whittier tried writing it down, but it was not to be finished until nearly thirty years later. This gestation period proved valuable, for when Whittier finally wrote "Skipper Ireson's Ride" he created the best American ballad of the nineteenth century.

The ballad opens slowly, almost incongruously, as the strangeness of Ireson's ride out of Marblehead is compared to other famous rides of story and rhyme. The reference to Apuleius' journey after his transformation into an ass, to Mohammed's flight on the back of a strange winged, white mule, and to the Tartar king's ride on a magical horse of brass, are purposefully outlandish and, as George Arms has pointed out, set a grotesque, grimly humorous tone for the opening stanzas. The refrain, which is repeated with slight variations in every stanza, gives the essence of the story, though it does not tell why the skipper is being punished. The second and third stanzas put the reader immediately *in medias res* as we watch the tarred and feathered captain driven through the streets of Marblehead by the enraged populace. The descriptions are exaggerated, even ludicrous, for Floyd's dishevelled condition is mocked as "Body of turkey, head of owl,/Wings a-droop like a rained-on fowl" and later on as "an Indian idol glum and grim." The crowd, strangely consisting of women, responds to his plight with raucous cries and violent jostling which travesty the underlying seriousness of the scene. Their wild actions create a half-mad, half-comic mood which catches the chaos and confusion of mob action. Again the comparisons follow a classical pattern as the recklessness of the girls in the crowd is portrayed:

> Wild-eyed, free-limbed, such as chase
> Bacchus round some antique vase,
> Brief of skirt, with ankles bare,
> Loose of kerchief and loose of hair,
> With conch-shells blowing and fish-horns' twang,
> Over and over the Maenads sang.

The reference to the frenzied antics of Bacchus' women followers links Ireson's present misery to the ancient accounts of males being torn to pieces during the orgies of the Maenads. From another aspect it also ridicules the pathetic figure of Ireson who is far from being the jovial god of wine and farther from enjoying the rite now being performed in his honor.

The tone changes in the fourth and fifth stanzas as the reasons for the punishment are revealed. He had sailed away from a sinking ship that was filled with his own townspeople; he had betrayed his own kin. The brief dialogue in stanza four gives the crucial moment of the tragedy, as the drowning crew called out for Ireson to save them, only to receive his heartless reply, "Sink or swim!/Brag of your catch of fish again!" Only this and nothing more. We never know his motivation, nor is the event further elaborated. One can surmise from the tone of fragmentary conversation that there was a deep-rooted enmity between Floyd and the crew over a catch of fish, and for this he wrathfully allowed them to die. The horror of his act is enlarged upon by the pathetic picture of the women of Marblehead, looking "for the

70

coming that might not be." Now we know why the women pursue the old skipper—they are the dead men's wives, mothers, sisters, and daughters, trying to wring some measure of revenge for the senseless death of their loved ones. Now we can understand why their actions are such a curious blend of humor and hate, for their disorder and emotional confusion symbolize their own broken lives. All these things are but touched upon as the story moves quickly back to the original scene and Ireson's shameful ride. Stanza six returns to the savage humor of the opening, rising to a climax with this description of the old men who join the women:

> Sea-worn grandsires, cripple-bound,
> Hulks of old sailors run aground,
> Shook head, and fist, and hat, and cane,
> And cracked with curses the hoarse refrain.

Part of Whittier's achievement is seen in these lines. The shipwreck images echo Ireson's betrayal and ridicule the pitiful attempts of the old sailors to obtain revenge, while their feeble, cracking voices make the refrain childish and meaningless. The crippled quality of their acts and the female character of the mob indicate the complete failure of the townspeople to obtain any measure of satisfaction that equals their loss.

Suddenly the mood shifts, and in contrast to the harsh voices of the turbulent mob in the narrow winding streets is the peace and serenity of the road leading to nearby Salem:

> Sweetly along the Salem road
> Bloom of orchard and lilac showed.
> Little the wicked skipper knew
> Of the fields so green and the sky so blue.

As the physical setting changes for artistic contrast, so does the psychological tone. For the first time the skipper is allowed to dominate the scene. Here again the action is presented through dialogue, rather than through author-narration, to preserve dramatic intensity. The outward scene fades, along with the ignominy of the ride and tarring, when the inward soul of the skipper cries out wretchedly:

> What to me is this noisy ride?
> What is the shame that clothes the skin
> To the nameless horror that lives within?

The transition is sudden and complete, surprising the reader who is engrossed in the outward narrative and making him startlingly aware of the poem's chief theme—the torture and remorse of a man after his crime. Though the hate of the mob and his present physical disfigurement will pass with time, his own terrible awareness of the sin will not. The image of the material clothes of shame (the tar and feathers) is contrasted with his mental revulsion for the crime, which covers or clothes his soul; the external suffering becomes insignificant when compared to the torments of conscience. Ireson's unexpected admission of guilt is perhaps unmotivated, but the change from hate to remorse is in keeping with the shifting pattern of the poem, its mixture of humor, pathos, and cruelty—all ironic paradoxes which highlight the irrationality of mob action and revenge. The crowd's response to Ireson's outcry attests to the validity of the skipper's comments; in accord with their New England religious heritage their vengeful yells turn to sorrowful murmurings. In "half scorn, half pity" they turn him loose and with a fine ironic echo of the clothes image give him a cloak to hide in. The final refrain changes "Old" Floyd Ireson to "Poor" Floyd Ireson and so becomes a mournful dirge forever accusing and dooming the man as well as emphasizing the hollowness remaining in the lives of the townspeople. The ballad makes Ireson live as an essentially tragic figure, a man who has betrayed the loyalties of his home and the manly traditions of the sea. He towers over the drama, coming from the sea, acting without apparent justification, and then vanishing to live alone with his shame.

The ballad succeeds because of its dramatic structure, sure handling of tone, definite localization, simplicity of diction, and knowledge of the psychology indigenous to New England. The whole poem centralizes on one incident, Skipper Ireson's ride from Marblehead. Like "Sir Patrick Spens," the well-known old English ballad, the story is based on a conflict of loyalties and gives no description of the central incident; the sinking of the ship is merely indicated by a brief dialogue, while its effects are seen in the actions of the townspeople. The tone is a unique blend of grim exaggeration, farfetched allusion, and genuine pathos which captures perfectly the swirl of conflicting emotions resulting from deep pain and sudden loss. Throughout, the author is impersonal, employing terse dialogue to keep the action objective and straightforward. And there is no moral attached, for it is organic within the story itself. The variations in the ballad, from the outward crowd scene to the flashback, then to the crowd again, and to the final sudden psychological twist, masterfully sustain interest. Whittier was to write other fine ballads—some more famous—but none were to equal the harmony of content and form which he achieved here.

◦§ §◦

At last Whittier had attained the artistry to express his feelings for the New England scene, its history, customs, and deeper psychological traditions. And so in rapid succession followed the gems of his maturity: the lyric drama "Telling the Bees"; the pastoral romance ballads "Amy Wentworth," "The Countess," and "The Witch of Wenham"; the hardier ballads of history and superstition "The Wreck of Rivermouth," "The Garrison of Cape Ann," and "The Palatine"; and his later dramatic ballads of Quaker persecution "The King's Missive" and "How the Women Went from Dover." Francis B. Gummere states in his introduction to *Old English Ballads* that spontaneity is one of the virtues of the ballad, that ballads never give "poetry for poetry's sake, but are born of an occasion, a need; they have as little subjectivity as speech itself." Whittier's most famous ballad, "Barbara Frietchie," exemplifies this phase of ballad approach. The incident—the courage of an old lady in waving a Union flag before the conquering rebel troops—was supposedly a true one. The poem was written in the heat of the crucial battle year of 1863 and embodied Whittier's passionate belief that fundamentally many southern rebels loved the Union as he did. His years of Abolitionist work had centered around a peaceful solution to the problem, but when the war came Whittier resigned himself to waiting and enduring its horrors. He knew that the Union must be preserved, and this poem was his spontaneous expression of that feeling. He saw in the image of Barbara Frietchie's holding the stars and stripes a symbol of all who loved the Union and were willing to die for it.

The story is told in the simplest of all verse forms, rhyming couplets of four beats a line, separated into stanzas. The rhythm has a biblical cadence and also catches the tramp of heavy boots as the rebels advance upon the town. The stage for the drama is set by the few suggestive details, evoking the environs of Frederick town and the luxuriant land, ripe both for the actual crop harvest and for the one of blood and destruction: "meadows rich with corn," and "apple and peach tree fruited deep." The action proper begins with the entrance of the "famished rebel horde" into the town and the disappearance of the Union flags:

> Forty flags with their silver stars,
> Forty flags with their crimson bars,
>
> Flapped in the morning wind: the sun
> Of noon looked down, and saw not one.

These lines have a perfect ballad movement, and a continuing economy of detail sweeps the drama along: the ranks of soldiers are "dust-brown"; and their leader, Stonewall Jackson, is characterized by his "slouched hat" and impetuous order to shoot the last flag down. Barbara Frietchie's act in waving the torn flag and her address to the rebels, "Shoot if you must this old grey head,/But spare your country's flag," are melodramatic, as are Jackson's blush of shame and order to his troops to spare the woman. Yet this unpolished and highly emotional presentation is in keeping with the manner of true balladry, where subtlety is a thing unknown. The theatrical nature of Barbara Frietchie's and Jackson's acts heightens the climax and pointedly illustrates the theme. Her successful defense of the flag is underscored by Whittier's picture of it waving over the heads of the rebel host and leads to the ending tribute, "Flag of Freedom and Union, wave!" The final couplets tightly bind the drama together as the stars of evening shine over the graves of the protagonists, the town, and the Union itself, suggesting nature's full approval of the battle for "peace and order and beauty" represented in the flag. By means of this simple story, Whittier echoed the thoughts and emotions of an entire country. No other Civil War poem, save Walt Whitman's "O Captain! My Captain!" and Julia Ward Howe's "Battle Hymn of the Republic," was so definitely the product of the hour and so quickly recognized by the people as an expression of their feelings.

≈§ §≈

Whittier's mature ballads show many interesting variations. "Amy Wentworth," like many others, is more a genre piece than a ballad, since it lacks dramatic action. The poem mainly portrays a tradition-reared Amy Wentworth who defies her rank to love a common sea captain. Its sentimental theme, the power of true love, is saved by the fine imagistic development of the poem. Amy's background is portrayed by the material objects which surround her, the beautiful piano, her silken dress, the stately stairway, the ancestral portraits in the hall, and the English ivy curving about the coat of arms. These externals are contrasted with her inner determination to love as she desires, not as the artifacts of tradition direct. Her physical beauty and the spirit of her love are captured by a series of sea images. The ballad opens with a graceful image of her fragile, delicate appearance and then continues with a more evocative sea image:

> Her fingers shame the ivory keys
> They dance so light along;
> The bloom upon her parted lips
> Is sweeter than the song.
>
> .   .   .   .   .   .
>
> Her heart is like an outbound ship
> That at its anchor swings;
> The murmur of the stranded shell
> Is in the song she sings.

The images in the second stanza thus center on the sea concept, the straining of an anchored ship and the helplessness of a washed-up shell. Like the shell, Amy is caught (stranded) by her ancestral background which forbade marriage outside its class, and she can only weakly murmur until her lover (the sea) sweeps her back into his grasp. The whole situation in the poem is summed up by the two words "stranded" and "murmur," which carry the subtle undertones of her longing and wistfulness. Throughout, this sea imagery is contrasted with the physical heaviness of her ancestral home and its precise refinement. Also her lover's voice, unlike hers, is sounded in the "clanging cry" of the white gulls and his rough jerkin gives a strength to her delicate silken gown. Striving to bring her absent lover closer, she imagines the house's gallery as his deck and finds pebbles and sand more attractive than her family's garden. The whole poem preserves this air of fragile romantic beauty so rarely found in Whittier's poems.

Sections of "The Witch of Wenham" and "How the Women Went from Dover" contain some of Whittier's best rendering of Colonial customs and illustrate his complete understanding of the psychology of witchcraft and local superstition. However, over-long digressions and sentimental touches mar the graphic descriptions and rustic phrases—indicating again how badly Whittier's art suffered from a lack of selection. "The Palatine" also catches the grim and foreboding atmosphere of past days in recording the legend of a spectre ship. Throughout there is swiftness of narrative and the ending remarks avoid Whittier's usual moralizing to hint at the complexity existing between the physical and spiritual worlds. In the ending conceit Whittier wonders if the return of the ship to haunt those who wrecked it isn't nature's grim comment on our past actions:

> Do the elements subtle reflections give?
> Do pictures of all the ages live
> On Nature's infinite negative,
>
> Which, half in sport, in malice half,
> She shows at times, with shudder or laugh,
> Phantom and shadow in photograph?

Two of Whittier's less well known ballads also merit attention. "The Sisters" is based on a traditional ballad theme—the rivalry of two sisters for the same man—and bears a close resemblance to the original Scottish ballad "The Twa Sisters" in form and presentation. The action of the story is concentrated on a single stormy night as the sisters sleep. Annie, the younger, awakens and hears a voice calling to her. From here the narrative drives forward without a pause. The love conflict and the impending tragedy are hinted at by Rhoda's scornful attitude toward the voices and by her derisive remarks about Annie's failure to have a lover. Ironically, she hits upon the truth of the situation when she ridicules Annie's insistence that she does hear the voice of Estwick Hall, Rhoda's fiancé. When Annie claims to hear the voice again calling her name, the now enraged sister cries out:

> "Thou liest! He would never call thy name!
>
> "If he did, I would pray the wind and sea
> To keep him forever from thee and me!"

76

Again Rhoda unwittingly keynotes the approaching tragedy, for Hall is dead. Only Annie, with her lover's insight, knows the truth, and in his death she triumphs as she never could have had he lived. She faces her sister and for the first time reveals her feelings:

> "Life was a lie, but true is death.
>
> .   .   .   .   .   .
>
> But now my soul with his soul I wed;
> Thine the living, and mine the dead!"

The whole narrative is done in dialogue with none of the before- or after-events included. Only the one scene is given, the resulting effects of the tragedy, and the reader himself must fill in the details. The presentation is bare, almost harsh, in its simplicity. Still, the story is definitely tied up with the New England coast, not as in so many literary ballads situated in the land of romance: the storm which drowns Hall is a typical New England northeaster; the waves lash Cape Ann's rocky coast; and the girls' dialogue has a New England flavor, for Hall's boat is the "tautest schooner that ever swam" and Rhoda's trousseau is "bridal gear."

Another of Whittier's later pieces, "The Henchman" (1877), also demonstrates his mastery of ballad techniques. Like "The Sisters," it has no moral, but it is entirely different in tone and presentation. The poem is a love song, chanted exultantly and hopefully by the lover in praise of his lady. The imagery centralizes on the joyous things of spring and summer, birds, flowers, sun, and wind, and makes the lady superior to them all.

> My lady walks her morning round,
> My lady's page her fleet greyhound,
> My lady's hair the fond winds stir,
> And all the birds make songs for her.
>
> .   .   .   .   .   .
>
> The hound and I are on her trail,
> The wind and I uplift her veil;
> As if the calm, cold moon she were,
> And I the tide, I follow her.

The repetition of certain phrases and syntactical patterns conveys the reverence of the lover's devotion with a litany of praise. The action of the ballad is slight, though there is an undercurrent of conflict—his adoration versus her proud disdain. However, this is never developed and the lyric and decorative effects dominate.

This type of ballad is the exception rather than the rule for most of Whittier's later pieces. Some of his mature ballads, such as "The Brown Dwarf of Rügen," "King Volmer and Elsie," and "Kallundborg Church," also convey the charm of a foreign land and create a fairy tale atmosphere by the techniques used in "The Henchman"; in general, however, Whittier's later ballads tend to take a concrete historical incident or some local tradition and dramatize it, using actual locale for realistic background setting. These tales fit in perfectly with his critical belief that there is romance underlying the simplest of incidents and that the writer should utilize the materials within his own experience.

✺   ✺

"The Wreck of Rivermouth" is typical. The story is based on the historical character of Goody Cole of Hampton, who was persecuted for being a witch in the latter half of the seventeenth century. Many of the exploits attributed to her were probably superstitions based on unfounded popular traditions; yet they were common in Whittier's youth. The setting is laid precisely, with an eye for picturesque detail:

> And fair are the sunny isles in view
>   East of the grisly Head of the Boar,
> And Agamenticus lifts its blue
>   Disk of a cloud the woodlands o'er;
> And southerly, when the tide is down,
> 'Twixt white sea-waves and sand-hills brown,
> The beach-birds dance and the gray gulls wheel
> Over a floor of burnished steel.

The ballad proper begins with the boat full of "goodly company," sailing past the rocks for fishing outside the bay. The idyllic atmosphere of the summer's day is conveyed by the picture of the mowers in the Hampton meadows, who listen to the songs coming from the passing boat and who longingly watch the joyous young girls. As the boat rounds the point where Goody Cole lives, the laughing group taunts her and sails on, but only after she answers their jibes with a bitter proverb: " 'The broth will be cold that waits at home;/For it's one to go, but another to come!' " Ironically her prophecy proves true, as a sudden storm sweeps upon the ship, driving it to destruction on Rivermouth Rocks. In one brief moment all are lost, and the next stanzas mournfully re-echo their previous happiness; the mower still looks up from the peaceful meadows and the sea is clear, but

> The wind of the sea is a waft of death,
>   The waves are singing a song of woe!
> By silent river, by moaning sea,
> Long and vain shall thy watching be:
> Never again shall the sweet voice call,
> Never the white hand rise and fall!

A stunned and broken Goody Cole is left behind, pathetically cursing the sea for fulfilling her wish. Her tragedy, like Skipper Ireson's, is an inner thing—the torment she will have for the rest of her life, wondering if her angry words actually caused the death of the group. The final scene in church highlights the community's silent condemnation of those who dare to live outside its conventions. This scene is overlong and weakened by the needless introduction of another outcast, Reverend Stephen Bachiler, and by the heavy moral tone of the conclusion, "Lord, forgive us! we're sinners all!"

The poem illustrates Whittier's successes and failures in ballad presentation. The story itself is typical and probable, and Whittier's handling of it is realistic. He places it exactly in Hampton, New Hampshire, by employing details characteristic of that locale: fishing for haddock and cod, the scent of the pines of nearby Rye, the mowing of salted grass, and Goody Cole's use of familiar native proverbs. There is a keynote of drama in the situation and a direct narrative appeal that fit ballad presentation, for Whittier allows us to view a most human Goody Cole, an old woman tragically destroyed by a village's narrow hate. Yet, like so many of Whittier's ballads, this one needs more concentration, especially in ending before the dramatic effect is lost. Also, there is a touch here of his overreaching for sentimental and melodramatic effects, a fault clearly seen in "The Changeling" and "How the Women Went from Dover."

On the whole, Whittier's ballads demonstrate his pioneer work in the development of native American ballads. He understood the true function of balladry and refused to write ballads based on European themes. Whittier took moments from American history and local legends and presented them in a realistic manner that was strengthened by his wide knowledge of past times and his lifelong familiarity with the locale. In these ballads Whittier attained the rank of one of America's finest creators of historical and traditional narrative.

7

ৰ৾ GENRE POETRY

THE DISTINCTION between Whittier's sectional or genre poems and his ballads is often nonexistent. Many poems such as "Telling the Bees" (discussed in chapter five), "Amy Wentworth" (discussed in chapter six), and "Maud Muller" can be handled either as ballads or genre poems. Usually the genre verses differ from the ballads in their lack of drama and objectivity; they are personal and subjective, fully revealing the poet and his ideas. Their subject matter deals with the life and manners of common people, a recollection of a past agrarian society or a nostalgic remembrance of boyhood experiences. Often they are longer, employing description and decorative imagery which minimize physical action and narrative pace, and the tone of wistful longing and romantic reminiscence replaces the impersonality and directness of the ballad. The best genre poems realistically portray the particular scenes, customs, traditions, and personages of nineteenth-century rural New England: the fields, drab and bare on a sleety winter day or green and growing under a summer sun; the plain Colonial houses with their massive cross beams, wide fireplaces, and rustic furniture; the barns filled with harvest or the excitement of a husking party; the isolation and narrowness of a small town with its delight in superstitions, eccentric wanderers, and local poets; the emotional effect of evangelical preaching on a farm populace; the traditional folk tales of stern "Yankee" forebears—the list is seemingly endless, a complete social history of the period. These genre poems most vividly exemplify Whittier's belief that the best materials for poetry lie in the commonplace objects of familiar experience.

Whittier's achievement in these poems goes beyond that of the mere local colorist who emphasizes regional peculiarities and the strangely picturesque or who produces folklore sketches and antiquarian pieces. Of course Whittier depends on his home territory for the images and situations of his genre art, but in his best Essex County poems the life of the region becomes the medium for his expression of universal insights and attitudes. His genre poems illustrate the validity of Frederick Jackson Turner's remark that "American literature is not a simple thing, but the choral song of many sections." This regional diversity not only preserves a section's own characteristics and history, but gives vitality and flavor to the nation's literature.

ও৽ ৈ৵

"Maud Muller" shows Whittier's genre art at its most typical. The story is an unpretentious account of the popular American belief in romantic love, set in a quaint rural background; yet Whittier pauses in the poem to examine realistically this trust and to question its validity. The poem's narrative sparseness and ironic undertones avoid his usual sentimentality and overelaboration. The occasion for the poem was Whittier's recollection of a trivial event—his meeting with a young farm girl and her shame at her torn attire and bare feet. To this matter-of-fact incident Whittier added an unadorned story of the appearance of a wealthy judge and the effect of this meeting upon their lives. The surface theme illustrates the belief that instinctive romantic love is the only basis for happiness, but for once Whittier undercuts excessive sentiment by ironic development of the theme and realistic presentation of the action. The structure of the poem is built upon a series of contrasts, of reality versus the dream and of action versus thought. As George Arms has pointed out, the opening stanzas prepare for an objective treatment of the romance. Whittier has the "mock-bird" echoing Maud's daydreams, and the town she gazes at, the symbol of her romantic aspirations, is "far-off" and only causes her "vague unrest" and unhappiness. The judge appears seated on his horse, while Maud blushingly offers him a cup of water. This simple placement of figures quietly indicates their basic, unreconcilable differences. After her meeting with him, Maud sighs wistfully, "Ah, me!/That I the Judge's bride might be" and naively dreams of the fine dresses and social benefits that would derive from the marriage. The judge is also considering marriage with her but from an entirely different aspect, wishing that he might live the simple life of a farmer, close to nature without the problems of his present social position. Each desires what the other one has, and each is temporarily affected by the power of the wish: the judge hums a tune in court and Maud leaves the hay unraked. However, their dreams fade in the hard light of reality. The judge marries within his own class, though he constantly remembers and idealizes the former meeting. As he drinks a glass of wine, he longs for Maud's cool drink. Maud fares even worse. Instead of living in a fine house with the handsome judge for her husband, she dwells in a cramped hovel as the wife of a poor, coarse farmer; yet she refuses to let the past die and continually relives the meeting, envisioning her unattractive kitchen walls as "stately halls." The concluding moral grows directly out of the story; it is the quiet musing of the author as he looks back on the dreams of all youths and realizes that "of all sad words of tongue or pen,/The saddest are these: 'It might have been!'" As viewed within the context of the poem, the "sadness" of this tale lies not in their failure to marry, but in their refusal to confront reality. The imaginative hopes of the judge and Maud reflect the sentiments of the "rags to riches" saga and trust in romantic love; yet the poem warns that, although one may believe in and cherish the dream, reality and life usually prove different. The ending remarks probe deeper as Whittier points out that only in heaven may our human dreams be realized (and even here the subjunctive "may" indicates his doubt that heaven would consist of such romantic fulfillment) and that only a final spiritual goal provides consolation, not vain regrets. Rather than asking for a sentimental response to the story, Whittier indicates his doubts and asks the question, "Who knows what is best after all?"—and therewithin lie the pathos and universality of the tale.

The extreme plainness of the poem's diction is most noticeable. The words are mainly monosyllables, while the imagery is commonplace and undeveloped. The girl is portrayed by the most conventional terms: her eyes are long-lashed and innocent; she has a graceful air, a fair form, and a sweet face; the only touch of imagery in her description, her glowing with the *"wealth/*Of simple beauty and rustic health"* (italics mine) provides an ironic reflection on her impossible dreams. Characterization of the judge, too, is kept vague; the single adjective applied to him is "manly." Both the judge and Maud are types, symbols of the dreams of all mankind. Still the structure of the story is firmly ribbed with realistic setting, probable attitudes, and plausible action. The girl's dreams are the naive, unaffected ones of a farmer's daughter: she longs for fine dresses, jewels, and rich furnishings—her unsophisticated view of what wealth implies; characteristically, she would help all her relatives and give money to the poor. Her conversation with the judge revolves around the everyday things of her life—birds, trees, the haying, and the weather. Also the ending section on Maud's poverty-stricken existence discloses all the drabness and bitterness of her life. The poem is a classic of its kind in simplicity, for Whittier manipulates theme and story into an organic whole to keep sentiment at a distance.

&§ §&

Just as he captured the naive aspirations of his age, Whittier also preserved the memories of the old order and the history of the local scene. His rustic anecdotes, "Yankee" character sketches, and humorous satires of legends and superstitions have been almost completely neglected by critics; yet they rank with his finest poetic achievements. His fanciful handling of Cotton Mather's history of a fabled two-headed snake in "The Double-Headed Snake of Newbury" is a minor comic triumph. Whittier ridicules Mather's credulous account of the "wonder workings of God's providence" by thoroughly reworking the tale with appropriate exaggeration and a mock-heroic tone that satirize the Puritan delight in superstition and moralizing. The section on the townspeople opens with a description of the ancient gossips who, "shaking their heads in their dreary way," humorously parallel the coiling of the snake. The passage reaches a climax with Whittier's caricature of Cotton Mather's entrance:

> Cotton Mather came galloping down
> All the way to Newbury town,
> With his eyes agog and his ears set wide,
> And his marvelous inkhorn at his side;

> Stirring the while in the shallow pool
> Of his brains for the lore he learned at school,
> To garnish the story, with here a streak
> Of Latin and there another of Greek.

Even the ending of the poem preserves the burlesque mood as Whittier records the present-day life of the snake in a native proverb dealing with the quarreling of husband and wife: "One in body and two in will,/The Amphisbaena is living still." This poem is the best among a group including "The Preacher," "Birchbrook Mill," and "The Prophecy of Samuel Sewall."

ᦸᏕ Ꮦᦸ

Whittier never had notable success with characterization, but in a few anecdotes of historical figures that strikingly foreshadow the work of Robert Frost and Edwin Arlington Robinson he did capture the essential characteristics of the New England mind. "Abraham Davenport" shows Whittier's genre art at its most realistic and enjoyable. The "old preaching mood" of the poem is at once dryly humorous and honestly respectful. Whittier pictures Davenport's granite-like determination and shrewd common sense as he calmly goes about his legislative duties amidst the fear and religious hysteria occasioned by an eclipse of the sun, the famous dark day of 1780. The poem opens with a laconic observation on the present age's slackness:

> In the old days (a custom laid aside
> With breeches and cocked hats) the people
> Sent their wisest men to make the public laws.

The terror of the day, lampooned by the overdrawn setting and the farfetched comparisons, conveys the still strong Calvinist belief in a wrathful God and the presence of the supernatural in physical occurrences. As Howard Mumford Jones notes, the style with its "fusion of low relief with salient observations" keeps this formal description from being melodramatic.

> Birds *ceased* to sing, and all the barn-yard fowls
> *Roosted;* the cattle at the pasture bars
> *Lowed,* and *looked* homeward; bats on leathern wings
> *Flitted* abroad; the sounds of labor *died;*
> Men *prayed,* and women *wept.*
>
> (Italics mine.)

85

The humorous urgency of the verbs and the incongruity of such insignificant details only ridicule the total solemnity of the event to make the ending human prayers and tears outrageously anti-climactic. Emphasizing the lawgivers, "dim as ghosts," trembling beneath their formal legislative robes, the next section evokes the image of these men in their winding sheets and provides an ironic contrast with the previous picture of the wrathful God and his "inexorable Law." Their decision to adjourn introduces Abraham Davenport who rises, "slow cleaving with his steady voice/The intolerable hush." In a common sense blend of faith and realism he advises them: " 'Let God do His work, we will see to ours./Bring in the candles.' And they brought them in." The simple repetition of the thought again puts a humorous, yet authentic, perspective on the whole scene. So, by the flickering candlelight the apprehensive legislators debate "an act to amend an act to regulate/The shad and alewive fisheries." The complete incongruity of the bill with the scene is reinforced by the monotonous phrasing and repetition. Whittier can even afford a pun as he pictures his hero speaking "straight to the question, with no figures of speech/Save the ten Arab signs." In the midst of this scene Davenport stands as a figure of awe and grandeur:

> Erect, self-poised, a rugged face, half seen
> Against the background of unnatural dark,
> A witness to the ages as they pass,
> That simple duty hath no place for fear.

The concluding lines again echo the failure of the present day to develop such men.

⋑ ⋐

"Cobbler Keezar," "The Sycamores," and "Abram Morrison" also exemplify Whittier's facility in rustic character sketches. All three employ a ballad form and might well be classified as such. Two of the poems contrast song- and wine-loving immigrant outsiders, a German cobbler and an Irish workman, with the grim, repressed existence of the early Puritan settlers; and "Abram Morrison" follows the career of an Irish Quaker well known in Whittier's youth. All three poems are filled with Whittier's native wit and dry turn of phrase. One other characterization, "A Spiritual Manifestation," reveals a most human Roger Williams who

86

laconically depicts the mob of dissenters and religious cranks who formerly descended upon his colony:

> I hear again the snuffled tones,
>   I see in dreary vision
> Dyspeptic dreamers, spiritual bores,
>   And prophets with a mission.
>
> .   .   .   .
>
> I fed, but spared them not a whit;
>   I gave to all who walked in
> Not clams and succotash alone,
>   But stronger meat of doctrine.
>
> I proved the prophets false, I pricked
>   The bubble of perfection,
> And clapped upon their inner light
>   The snuffers of election.

The burlesque tone is heightened by Whittier's feminine rhymes and dialect associations such as "assorter–water" and "braggarts –fagots." Unfortunately, he did not let Williams' monologue stand by itself but apologized for his "light" treatment of the reformer—once again illustrating Whittier's distressing lack of artistic control and inability to condense. These failings are also evident in "To My Old Schoolmaster" and "The Prophecy of Samuel Sewall," where realistic genre touches, shrewd social comment, and character insight are obscured by didactic passages and digressive material.

⊸§ §⊷

More and more Whittier turned to the memories of his own youth for poetic material, typifying and idealizing the barefoot days, the district school days, and lost childhood romances. Throughout all these poems run the strains of his sentimental longing for the simplicity of a past social order. "The Barefoot Boy," "In School-Days," "My Playmate," "Memories," and "A Sea Dream" captured the romantic aspirations of a wide reading public and were enshrined as part of traditional Americana along with Longfellow's verses, the songs of Stephen Foster, and Emanuel Leutze's painting of "Washington Crossing the Delaware." Though "The Barefoot Boy" displays Whittier's most obvious artistic flaws, it also indicates why his verses were so popular. The introduction is sentimental and unreal, depending on hackneyed imagery and conventional poetic diction. The boy is styled "little man," wears "pantaloons," has lips "kissed by strawberries on the hill," and is pompously addressed as "Prince." These generalizations reveal nothing about a real boy or his background; rather they show how responsive Whittier was to the Currier and Ives's approach to local color. The central section of the poem does realistically examine the world and interests of a small boy. Forgetting the idealized little man, Whittier identifies himself with the scene:

> I was rich in flowers and trees,
> Humming-birds and honey-bees;
> For my sport the squirrel played,
> Plied the snouted mole his spade;
> For my taste the blackberry cone
> Purpled over hedge and stone.
>
> .   .   .   .   .   .
>
> All the world I saw or knew
> Seemed a complex Chinese toy,
> Fashioned for a barefoot boy!

The last stanzas return to the platitudes of the opening as Whittier concludes with the pious hope that the boy's bare feet will never sink in the "quick and treacherous sands of sin." And yet this poem became a national tradition, symbolizing a romantic phase of America's past. Its companion piece, "In School-Days," is correctly considered a poem for children, though its first four stanzas do contain some of Whittier's best local color description. "My Playmate" is the best of the three love lyrics which nostalgically recall the bittersweet pain of young love. Its blend of memory and reality, symbolized by the moaning pines and falling blossoms, artistically portrays an older man's sense of regret and longing.

ᦥ ᦥ

One of Whittier's most neglected poems, "The Pennsylvania Pilgrim," shows how accurately and realistically he could re-create the past. His portrait of the seventeenth-century Quaker Pastorius fully explores the varied nature of that settler, while the mood and imagistic development of the poem convey Pastorius' quiet, secure personality. The "Prelude" establishes the poem's contemplative mood with its emphasis on Pastorius as a pilgrim of "a softer clime/And milder speech" who lives completely by the "white" radiance of the Inner Light. Its concluding lines introduce the other principal image of sowing and reaping.

Employing a style similar to Jonathan Edwards' *Personal Narrative* with its insistent repetition of certain phrases, Whittier connotes the presence of the Inner Light in Pastorius. Throughout the poem terms such as peace, mild, meek, simple, tender, sober, mystical, and others are continually enlarged upon and reechoed. Decorative, pastoral similes pervade the whole poem and create a quiet, almost dreamlike, atmosphere. Rarely did Whittier achieve a more artistic fusion of his own interests and those of the actual story than in the following lines:

> Fair First-Day mornings, steeped in summer calm,
> Warm, tender, restful, sweet with woodland balm,
> Came to him, like some mother-hallowed psalm
>
> .   .   .   .
>
> There, through the gathered stillness multiplied
> And made intense by sympathy,
>
> .   .   .   .
>
> Or, without spoken words, low breathings stole
> Of a diviner life from soul to soul,
> Baptizing in one tender thought the whole.

In the descriptions of Pastorius' silence as "soul-sabbath" or his reading the Bible by the "Inward Light," Whittier movingly and thoughtfully symbolizes the guiding force of Pastorius' Quaker faith. The climax to this light image comes with Whittier's paraphrase of Ezekiel's strange vision of the wheels, which is introduced:

> The Light of Life shone round him; one by one
> The wandering lights, that all-misleading run,
> Went out like candles paling in the sun.

Balancing this light image are references to planting, sowing, reaping, and blossoming which signify Pastorius' attempts to transplant Old World culture in the New, his cultivation of religious tolerance, and his work to free the slaves. In particular the image of the aloe or legendary plant that supposedly bloomed

John Greenleaf Whittier

every hundred years evokes the slow, patient efforts of Pastorius to make the Quakers renounce slavery. Whittier notes how this "seed of truth" does finally blossom under the hands of Woolman and other Quakers. The poem not only depicts Pastorius as the saint figure, but humanizes him by portraying the tender relationship between Pastorius and his wife, his tenacious fight for tolerance and abolishment of slavery, his speculative interests in science and religion, his monumental verse writings in "Dutch, English, Latin, like the hash/Of corn and beans in Indian succotash," his nostalgic recollection of music-filled Christmases in Germany, his love of local superstition and Indian lore, and his achievement in transferring "the Old World flowers to virgin soil." The portrait leaves the reader with a full impression of a complex, idealistic, and learned Quaker who was at the same time a simple, tolerant, and humble man.

❧ ☙

The most famous of Whittier's genre poems, and undoubtedly his masterpiece, is "Snow-Bound." Written a few months after the end of the Civil War, it was Whittier's memorial to the two women who were closest to him during his life—his mother, who had died eight years before, and his sister Elizabeth, who had died the previous year. The loss of his favorite companion, Elizabeth, left Whittier a lonely man, and the outcome of the Civil War completed the one great work of his life. In this mood of sorrow and isolation, Whittier turned to the happy past when the family was intact at the Haverhill birthplace, and constructed this winter idyl to express his feelings for the section and family which had produced and molded him. Its theme, the value of family affection, had always been deepest in his heart; and its locale, the homestead during a snowstorm, was one he knew intimately. Nowhere in Whittier's work, outside of some of his ballads, had the material so suited his capabilities and interest.

Relying on Whittier's comment that "Snow-Bound" portrays "Flemish pictures of old days," most critics have examined it as a loosely connected montage which quaintly evokes the atmosphere of rural New England in the 1800's.* Such comment accords value

* One notable exception is George Arms's excellent essay on Whittier. This analysis has utilized Arms's comments on the fire symbol, the antislavery theme, and the meaning of the "century's aloe" and has been further expanded by his personal criticism.

to Whittier's graphic rendering of physical details, to his authentic delineation of family figures, and to his fidelity to actual experience. But the poem, "old, rude-furnished" like the house, does burst "flower-like, into rosy bloom" and this artistic fruition is not a chance occurrence. The imagistic development of the poem, use of appropriate symbols, and closely organized structure provide a satisfying artistic framework for these rustic scenes. An examination of these aspects indicates a genuine literary value far beyond local or historical interest.

The theme turns on the poet's nostalgic recalling of the love and protection which his family once gave him, emphasizing his painful sense of present loss and hope for spiritual consolation. These emotions are primarily developed by a series of contrasts: of fire and snow, past and present, people and elements—which combine to form the larger theme of love and immortality struggling against pain and death.

Perhaps the touchstone for interpreting the poem is the symbolic development of the wood fire. The poem is headed by a quotation from Agrippa's *Occult Philosophy:* "As the Spirits of Darkness be stronger in the dark, so Good Spirits, which be Angels of Light, are augmented not only by the Divine light of the Sun, but also by our common Wood Fire: and as the Celestial Fire drives away dark spirits, so also this our Fire of Wood doth the same." Also a second epigraph from Emerson's "The Snow-Storm" re-emphasizes the importance of the "radiant" fire. In the poem, fire is associated not only with brightness, relaxation, and physical comfort, but with the emotional and spiritual warmth of family love, with "the genial glow" of community brotherhood, and with divine protection against the evil spirits of nature and time. Artistically delayed by the description of the "unwarming" storm, the initial lighting of the fire introduces the Whittier household, and its blaze symbolizes the reality of family love. Throughout the central section, particularly, Whittier associates the vigor and happiness of family talk, games, and interests with the color and sparkle of the glowing logs; and unites the close bond of family love with the red heat of the fire. For example, the uncle's simple tales are "warming" and cause the listeners to forget "the outside cold,/The bitter wind." Also Whittier weaves into the fire pattern the sunny richness, ripe crops, blooming hillsides, and full greenness associated with summer. Finally, the dying fire indicates the end of the evening's activities, while also symbolizing the eventual crumbling of the security and protection of the family group.

By contrast, the storm evokes sensations of fear and awe and illustrates the terrible anonymity of nature and death. It dominates the entire first section of the poem, transforming its principal antagonist, the sun, into a cheerless, dark, snowblown wanderer, and enforcing on the family a "savage" isolation which obtains no comfort from "social smoke." The storm's assault on the house is likened to the later attack of death on its individual members as Whittier recalls "the chill weight of the winter snow" on Elizabeth's grave. Conversely, the storm's magical power changes a dull, commonplace farm into a wintry fairyland of beauty and wonder.

A second major contrast deals with the past versus the present. Whittier imaginatively re-creates the past, while echoing his present-day feelings of loneliness. Four main interpolations deal with this problem of time and change, contrasting past happiness with present pain and concluding with the hope for future social progress and spiritual consolation. For example, the first interpolation (lines 179–211) appropriately comes when the fire is lighted and the storm's force seems abated. As if lost in the scene he has recalled, Whittier cries: "What matter how the night behaved?/What matter how the north-wind raved?" But immediately the knowledge of "Time and Change" stop him; for what the elements failed to do that night death has since accomplished. These stark reflections are contrasted with the strength of Whittier's faith as the section ends with his defiant affirmation that spiritual life is the "lord of Death," for a soul's love remains an eternal force. These major contrasts are further expanded by an increasing depth of images and a movement from concrete physical description to an investigation of personality and emotions, with a final return to realistic depiction. All these aspects are blended into the total theme—the strength and bond of family love.

Yet the underlying unity of the poem is developed by a time cycle—the two days' snowfall; the third day's activity and family gathering that night; the fourth day's visit of the teamsters and the doctor; and finally, after a week, the arrival of the newspaper, completely breaking the isolation. However, within this framework is a more ordered threefold division which pits the forces of nature against the family group. The first section of the poem (to line 178) presents the physical domination of the storm and concludes with a view of the inner house and the lighting of the fire. The emphasis throughout is on exact physical detail and on the primitive forces of nature. In the second section the storm is forgotten, for human love and companionship have exorcised the raging spirits of the night. The images become more complex and introspective as loneliness and nostalgia overwhelm the poet. The dying embers of the fire and dreams of summer open the third section (line 629) with a return to the outside physical world; correspondingly, the images also become more concrete. Here the theme of family strength is widened to the larger bond of community union. The final interpolation emphasizes the "larger hopes and graver fears" of social responsibility that can finally unite all mankind, just as the bond of personal love and Quaker Inner Light had once securely linked the Whittier family. This section closes with a hope that art will also preserve some of the more valued aspects of the family group.

A closer analysis of each section reveals the skillful interweaving of the theme with structure and its artistic expansion from major imagistic contrasts. The poem opens with a description of the approaching storm and its complete domination over the "Divine light of the Sun," which is darkly circled, barely able to diffuse a sad "light." Still, as a portent, the sun briefly foreshadows the coming fire of the hearth which does temporarily defeat the storm. A sense of unusual expectation grips the early lines and the cold checks the "circling race/Of lifeblood"—suggesting the eventual triumph of death over the family life. A following description of nightly chores deepens this mood by emphasizing the helplessness of all animate beings before the elements. Then the full fury of the storm breaks to create a chaos of whirling, blinding snow which destroys man's order and intelligent control. On the second morning:

> The old familiar sights of ours
> Took marvelous shapes; strange domes and towers
> Rose up where sty or corn-crib stood,
>
> .   .   .   .
>
> The bridle-post an old man sat
> With loose-flung coat and high cocked hat;

> The well-curb had a Chinese roof;
> And even the long sweep, high aloof,
> In its slant splendor, seemed to tell
> Of Pisa's leaning miracle.

The condensed details of pure fancy, clever allusion, and purposeful exaggeration evoke a childlike wonder and convey a panoramic view of the transforming power of the storm. Once more human activity intrudes as the father and boys cut through "the solid whiteness" to reach the barn, but now even labor is a delight, for their finished tunnel resembles the dazzling crystal of Aladdin's cave. These pleasing aspects of the storm are immediately counterbalanced by a piercing wind which creates a "savage" world of terror and sunlessness, eliminates "social smoke," and deadens Christian sounds.

When the snowblown and still helpless sun sets that afternoon, loving hands gather the wood and brush necessary to kindle the fire. The "curious art" displayed in these simple tasks suggests a ritual-like significance in their performance. The first red blaze metamorphoses the kitchen into "rosy bloom," but an even greater miracle occurs as the snowdrifts outside reflect the inner fire with their own mimic flame. For the first time the fire controls and the snow receives its burning imprint. Yet the outer elements are not so easily conquered and the moon that night reveals an eerie half-world of "dead white" snows and "pitchy black" hemlocks suffused by an "unwarming" light. Once more the fire's "tropic heat" asserts its power and the glowing light reveals a mug of simmering cider, rows of apples, and a basket of nuts—objects closely associated with the inner world of personality and life.

Though the second section of the poem opens with an emphatic defiance of the elements, this confidence is soon undercut by the painful realization that time has finally conquered. For the faces "lighted" by love and the warmth of the fire are no longer alive ("in the sun they cast no shade"). Ironically, this realization occurs just as the fire does finally dominate the outside elements. Still, forcing these melancholy thoughts from mind by utilizing the fire–snow contrast, Whittier insists that the light of breaking day will play across the mournful marbles of the tomb—that love and faith will find spiritual happiness. This consolation provides an uneasy truce which allows the poet to describe the personalities of the family. The father, mother, and uncle are fittingly charac-

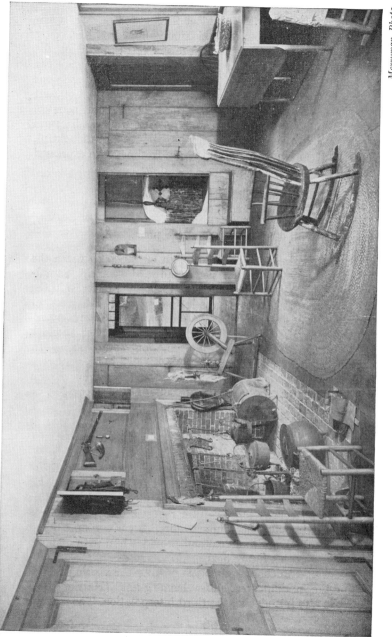

The Kitchen, Whittier's Birthplace at Haverhill

terized by warm summer days, outdoor fishing and haying, ripening corn, steaming clambakes, and sunny hillsides. Also their plain childlike natures and interests are perfectly echoed by the quaint couplet rhythm, the rough unpolished lines, and the vernacular "Yankee" rhymes. To follow these three innocent characters, Whittier introduces another group of three, the aunt and two sisters, whose more complex natures reflect some measure of life's pain, sacrifice, and loneliness. Similarly, the tone becomes more introspective and the images more expansive and thoughtful. The aunt's still youthful charm and virgin freshness are expressed in a delicate summer figure of clouds and dew:

> Before her still a cloud-land lay,
> The mirage loomed across her way;
> The morning dew, that dries so soon
> With others, glistened at her noon.

The elder sister's death is described as an entrance "beneath the low green tent/Whose curtain never outward swings." Significantly her death is not snow-filled or chilling; rather it is the casual lifting of a tent-flap with the later discovery that this light opening has now been closed with the heavy weight of "low green" sod. A following passage on Elizabeth, "our youngest and our dearest," introduces the second interpolation (lines 400–437). Once again Whittier's faith struggles with the brutal reality of death as the chilling snows of the grave cover the summer charm and violet beauty of Elizabeth's nature. Finally the poet asks:

> Am I not richer than of old?
> Safe in thy immortality,
> What change can reach the wealth I hold?

At first glance the figure appears paradoxical, for how can Elizabeth's death make the poet "richer" and "safe"? On one level his rich memories of her vibrant personality and spiritual perfection are now "safe," secured forever from realistic tarnish and inexorable change; but also her "immortality" secures him, since it illuminates his final spiritual goal and provides him with a standard for judging all his future acts.

The following two characterizations portray the visiting schoolmaster and the "not unfeared, half-welcome guest" (Harriet Livermore), while also introducing the third interpolation. The realistic sketch of the schoolmaster's entertaining knowledge of the classics and rural games, his boyish humor, and self-reliant, yet humble, nature is a fine genre portrait that matches the earlier ones of the father and uncle. Indeed the schoolmaster's close intimacy with the family is underscored by the lines that introduce him as one who "held at the fire his favored place,/Its warm glow lit a laughing face." His further delineation as one of "Freedom's young apostles" completes Whittier's portrait of the fearless young leader whose moral strength will destroy social injustice such as slavery and open a new era of peace and progress. At the same time the expansion of these optimistic ideas on the power of education and reform, in the third interpolation (lines 485–509), displays the thinness of Whittier's social thought; and its abstract, hackneyed imagery ("War's bloody trail," "Treason's monstrous growth") contrasts unfavorably with the concrete detail of other sections. The final figure, Harriet Livermore, presents an interesting variation of the fire imagery as she combines characteristics of both the spirits of light and blackness. Her warm and lustrous eyes flash light, but also hold "dark languish" and wrath; her brows are "black with night" and shoot out a "dangerous light." This tortured nature warps and twists the "Celestial Fire," for she enters the family group without sharing its close affection or receiving the warm benefits of love from the wood fire. Her complex characterization is appropriately climaxed by the uneasy observation that in some natures the line between "will and fate" is indistinguishable. Structurally these two outsiders represent the contrasting "warm–cold" aspects of a forgotten external world. The schoolmaster offers the warmth of companionship, the balance of learning, and eventual hope for social responsibility, while Harriet Livermore reveals the chill of fanaticism and the failure of personal, emotional efforts to correct injustice. Also their intrusion foreshadows the unavoidable demands that society is soon to make upon the secure family group.

Appropriately, the second section concludes when the family disbands for bed and the now dull fire is extinguished. As the family falls asleep, the snow sifts through the loosened clapboards and the storm re-enters the poem (though significantly the snow no longer has the power to disturb their dreams of summer). The ending of the night's activities carefully reworks the fire image:

> At last the great logs, crumbling low,
> Sent out a dull and duller glow,
> The bull's-eye watch that hung in view,
> Ticking its weary circuit through,
> Pointed with mutely warning sign
> Its black hand to the hour of nine.
> That sign the pleasant circle broke:
> My uncle ceased his pipe to smoke,
> Knocked from its bowl the refuse gray,
> And laid it tenderly away;
> Then roused himself to safely cover
> The dull red brands with ashes over.

The crumbling of the once great logs hints of nature's eventual triumph over the family unit, while the ominous black watch, like a living spirit of darkness, also specifies that time has run out. When the uncle knocks the ashes from his pipe, he deepens the suggestion of the burned-out logs and echoes the clock's warning. Even the halting verse pattern with its awkward inversions reflects the fumbling slowness and plodding, careful manner of the uncle.

The final section briefly returns to the physical world of the opening stanzas, as the teamsters and plows now control the effects of the storm, while the children find sport, instead of terror, in its whiteness. Signalizing the larger social union which radiates from the smaller family bond, the visiting doctor utilizes the mother's nursing skill to aid a sick neighbor. So love joins his "mail of Calvin's creed" with her Quaker "inward light." Finally, the local newspaper arrives and the family broadens its interests to other communities and "warmer" zones. Now the storm's isolation is completely broken and the section ends with the joyful cry, "Now all the world was ours once more."

While this seems to be the logical conclusion for the poem, it disregards the troubling theme of time's ultimate victory. So, in a final interpolation (from line 715) Whittier asks the "Angel of the backward look" to close the volume in which he has been writing. With difficulty he shakes off this mood of regret and nostalgia to respond to present-day demands (much as he had pictured the young schoolmaster doing) and employs the image of the century-blooming aloe to dramatically portray the successful flowering of his Abolitionist's aim to eradicate slavery. The ending lines further console Whittier with the hope that his "Flemish" artistry has truly re-created "pictures of old days" and that others might gather a similar spiritual and emotional comfort from them by stretching the "hands of memory forth/To warm them at the wood-fire's blaze!" A final summer image completes the poem as the thought of future readers enjoying his efforts refreshes him as odors blown from unseen meadows or the sight of lilies in some half-hidden pond. These lines reflect the inner serenity and imperturbable peace which offer final solace. The dread of time and change is assuaged by the confidence that social reform will improve the future, by the knowledge that art often outlasts time's ravages, and by the certainty that spiritual immortality does conquer it completely. So the poem moves in artistic transitions from the physical level of storm and fire to the psychological world of death and love, utilizing the wood fire as the dominant symbol. It is for this skillful fusing of form and theme that Whittier deserves that future readers send him "benediction of the air."

The interwoven theme and structure are enhanced by some of Whittier's finest genre touches. His descriptions of the homestead's kitchen, the fireplace, and his bedroom are imperishable vignettes which typify the thousands of similar New England farm houses. Throughout the poem there is an abundance of local color. The hake-broil on the beach and the chowder served with clam shells were part of a traditional New England clambake. The games of cross pins, forfeits, riddles, and whirling plate as well as the skating parties and husking bees were common rural practices. The family's activities and interests, fishing off the Isles of Shoals, hunting for teal and loon, trips to Salisbury and far-off Canada, tales of Indian raids, and delight in the almanac and weekly newspaper, were intimately connected with the New England scene. Even more particularized were the Quaker traits and practices detailed in the poem: their reading from Quaker journals, their practice of the Quaker doctrines of tolerance and spirituality, and their Quaker injunctions against slavery. If the Whittiers' interests and outlooks were those of an Essex County family in the early nineteenth century, from their definite local characteristics comes a broader picture of all New England and, indeed, all rural America at that time.

John Greenleaf Whittier

Like "Snow-Bound" the best of Whittier's genre poetry reflected the ideals and attitudes of the majority of the American public. His genre pieces captured their romantic dreams, belief in the value of the passing social order, deep-rooted religious faith, nostalgic recollection of childhood, and instinctive attachment to one locale. Throughout all these poems ran a distinctive local coloring in use of situation, description of scenery, and manner of expression, which made the themes concrete and probable. As Emerson embodied the philosophic thought of America in his poems, Whittier incorporated its common ideals and traditions in his. By being scrupulously true to his own experience, conscious of the beauty of the commonplace, and responsive to the popular sentiments of domesticity, piety, and freedom he was "the people's poet" in a sense that the educated and cultured genteel poets could never be.

8

৺৹ NATURE POEMS AND OTHERS

W HITTIER'S nature poetry was consistently handled in a
minor key—simply, directly, and pictorially. Unlike the
great Romantic writers Whittier could not respond lyrically or
sensuously to nature without the guilty feeling that he was neglecting man or morality. Though he deeply loved nature, he
strongly felt that "man was more than his abode," that natural
living without the practice and understanding of Christianity was
narrow and sinful, and that the Creator must always be perceived beneath the material splendor of nature. Usually Whittier
developed his nature description into a moral reflection about
man's spiritual being. Always he stressed nature's ability to soothe
his reformer's mind, handling it as a relaxing pause before his
return to the more important world of men and action. If the
nature poems were picturesque and romantic, their definite moral
core usually saved them from the age's sentimentality. Also limit-
ing his response to external beauty was his color blindness which
made his nature descriptions resemble etchings simply drawn in
lights and darks.

The opening lines of "The Prelude" to "Among the Hills" are
the outstanding exception to these generalizations:

Along the roadside, like the flowers of gold
That tawny Incas for their gardens wrought,
Heavy with sunshine droops the golden-rod,
And the red pennons of the cardinal-flowers
Hang motionless upon their upright staves.

The force and heat of the sun, its heavy gold effect, is developed
and expanded in perfect "imagist" fashion. The sun is pictured
as a palpable gold mass, pushing and crushing all the objects it
touches. The reference to the Incas' art work sets the heavy decorative effect of the scene, as the molten flow of sunshine oppresses the goldenrod and immures the resisting red pennons of
the cardinal flower into vertical stillness. The wind itself is "wing-
weary" and exhausted from its futile attempts to fan the sun,
while the cry of locusts must "stab" the silent burden of the
noon to be heard. The tone is hypnotic and languid, creating an
unreality which affects both humans and nature. The section closes
with a softer mood of drowsiness and sweet perfume to establish
a "pervading symphony of peace." This effective opening leads
into a brief consideration of the "Golden Age" possible under
such conditions (which is handled again at the conclusion of "The
Prelude") and it is contrasted with the adverse effects of this
same godlike sun. The weeds and desolation of an untilled garden,
the paint blistering on the walls, the dank fetid air of an enclosed
house, the listless atmosphere, symbolize the moral waste and
spiritual aridity of the inhabitants. These people are portrayed
with a realism and bite rarely found in Whittier's verse:

Blind to beauty everywhere revealed,
Treading the May-flowers with regardless feet;

.   .   .   .

Church goers, fearful of the unseen Powers,
But grumbling over pulpit-tax and pew-rent,
Saving, as shrewd economists, their souls
And winter pork with the least possible outlay
Of salt and sanctity.

ᡃᢌᡃᢈ ᢌᡃ

Two shorter poems show Whittier's more characteristic handling
of nature. "The Trailing Arbutus" unfolds in excellent imagistic
manner. The situation itself, the growth of this beautiful spring
flower amidst the barrenness of ending winter and receding snows,

contains the theme of the poem, the survival of beauty and goodness in the most "lowly" and "clogged" lives. The final stanza
where the meaning of the scene is applied to people's souls is not
just a moral tag, for the flower symbolizes the thought. All the
physical objects, the bitter eastern storms, the dead boughs, the
moaning pines, and dry leaves, which surround the budding flower
relate to the external human cold and desolation surrounding
people's lives. The poem grows as perfect lyric: the emotional,
sense-appealing content is fully developed in the first two stanzas;
the third reflects on the meaning of the scene.

"The Pressed Gentian" comments on a Christmas gift of a
flower enclosed in a window glass whose beauty is evident only to
those inside, for passing strangers see only the "dull blankness" of
glass. Whittier thoughtfully develops the implications of this
scene by a series of contrasts which move from the original image
of hidden physical beauty to the psychology of personal insight
into a soul's beauty and finally to a view of God's knowledge and
man's limitations. Throughout, the terms outside, stranger, cold,
sight, finite, and man are opposed to inner, friend, warmth, insight, infinite, and God. In a "Frostlike" manner Whittier explores
what insights a selfless human love can bring and how an added
spiritual perspective even approaches Divine knowledge. The
concluding moral comments that God alone can see the whole
soul and echoes the opening image of the poet sitting alone enjoying the hidden beauty of the flower.

Though Whittier's nature poems repeatedly dwell on warmth
and summertime, his most successful pieces usually describe the
starkness of fall or winter. "The Last Walk in Autumn" is undoubtedly his finest nature poem. Its opening stanzas graphically
render the oppressive quality of a gray, drab autumn day and
echo the poet's own sense of personal failure. The continuing survey of the same scene in different seasons leads into the theme of
the poem—why Whittier continues to stay in such a harsh climate
and why he loves this somber locale. The following lines illustrate
the sectional strength and inner sincerity that make Whittier's
better poems live today:

> Then ask not why to these bleak hills
> I cling, as clings the tufted moss,
> To bear the winter's lingering chills,
> The mocking spring's perpetual loss.

> I dream of lands where summer smiles
> And soft winds blow from spicy isles.
>
> .   .   .   .
>
> Better with naked nerve to bear
> The needles of this goading air.

❧ ☙

A group of openly introspective poems includes "Ego," sections of "The Tent on the Beach," "My Namesake," and "Proem" where Whittier reviews his life as a man and an artist. Awkward and halting as they may be, these poems do reveal the humble spirit of a man who dreamed of creating Spenser's "mystic beauty" only to see "the rigor of a frozen clime,/The harshness of an untaught ear," and his devotion to reform prevent such an achievement. In one of these introspective poems, "The Waiting," Whittier created his finest short lyric. The poem was nurtured during Whittier's thirty-year struggle for the peaceful settlement of the slavery problem and occasioned by his uneasy resignation to the resulting Civil War. He knew the Union must be preserved; yet his own pacifist Quaker principles heightened his paradoxical position—passionately desirous of Union victory while unable to justify the war itself or to aid those fighting. The tension of divided loyalties plagued him and he strove to resolve his doubts in this poem. As the poem opens, the poet is watching the first rays of the morning sun streak across the skies. He stands in their half-light (which reflects his own inner division), engrossed in his thoughts about the conflict. When he looks up, the jagged rays appear in form of golden spears, advancing under the banner of day (oriflamme) to conquer the enemy night. This martial image of movement is further developed in the second stanza as the "day-sounds swell and grow," moving quickly like troops in actual battle:

> Troop after troop, in swift advance,
> The shining ones with plumes of snow!

Now the mood changes (though two explicit references had previously prepared for this, the repetition of "I wait and watch" and the poet's picture of himself as "bound in trance"). With the mention of the "shining ones" the actual dawn scene is fully merged into the central drama of the poem—the action of those fighting and Whittier's detached position. He emphasizes the grandeur of the soldiers in battle by two motion images, "the errand of their feet" and "steps of progress," as a contrast to his own silent prayers which are formed with "unmeet" hands. In a despairing climax Whittier estimates his personal contribution:

> The puny leverage of a hair
> The planet's impulse well may spare,
> A drop of dew the tided sea.

The extent of his futility is suggested by the ironic disparity between the power of a true lever and one made of hair and the insignificance of a drop of dew in swelling a sea. The next lines offer paradoxical consolation to the poet:

> The loss, if loss there be, is mine,
> And yet not mine if understood.

To serve in one's own way and to the best of one's ability is not to be worthless, for "God shall make the balance good." This appears to be an easy reconciliation of his doubts to the will of God, but the final stanza, again introducing the motion image, concludes that "standing still" is harder than fighting. Understanding the problem and living with the horror of this knowledge is more difficult than escaping tension through physical action. The ending comments, that "good but wished with God is done," offer further religious comfort since one's final spiritual achievement will be measured in the objective light of eternity. In thirty packed lines the poem develops the image of physical action and battle into a searching examination of divided loyalties, contrasting the poet's outward waiting with his inner turmoil and final acceptance of God's will.

◅§ §▻

Most of the remainder of Whittier's occasional and personal poems are topical, conventionally phrased, and virtually unreadable today, but "Ichabod" and a few others merit attention: "To William Lloyd Garrison" catches the biblical fervor of that dedicated reformer; "Burns," though marred by didactic comments on Burns's life, does measure the extent of Burns's achievement in presenting the poetic beauty of the commonplace; and "Sumner" carefully works a statue image along with classical allusions to portray the awesome determination and loyalty that guided Sumner's life, while at the same time honestly noting his aloofness, pride, and lack of humor. Perhaps the best of the antislavery poems still have emotional appeal. Certainly the Hebraic fervor and passionate invective that fired Whittier's hatred of hypocrisy and oppression often transformed propaganda into poetry. Even today "Clerical Oppressors" and "Official Piety" can thrill although their historical occasion has long since been forgotten. For the modern reader the detached tone and satiric approach of "Lines on the Portrait of a Celebrated Publisher" and the down-East humor of "Letter from a Missionary . . ." are perhaps more appealing.

The one poem that rises to poetic immortality from this group is "Ichabod," which still remains one of the finest poems of invective ever written in America. It was occasioned by Whittier's shocked surprise and sudden sense of betrayal upon reading Daniel Webster's "Seventh Of March" speech in support of the Fugitive Slave Act. The intensity of Whittier's anger purged the topical nature of the poem, while his use of the Inner Light image to symbolize Webster's sin is masterfully sustained throughout. The very title of the poem has the biblical meaning of "inglorious one" and carries the suggestion of the fallen angels. The sharp, truncated first phrases, "So fallen! so lost!" startle as if wrenched from Whittier's soul, while the main metaphor is introduced by "the light withdrawn." Then the tone softens as Whittier mentions the "glory" which has departed from Ichabod's gray hairs and mournfully echoes his eternal damnation with the final word "Forevermore." At this point the reader does not know why Ichabod has lost the light, but he can understand that this light was a halo of goodness and beauty similar to that which once surrounded the fallen angels. The tone is a mixture of despair and bitter sorrow, a passion tempered by an awesome recognition of a soul's condemnation. Though marred by the trite image of the tempter, the mood of the second stanza, "pitying tears, not scorn and wrath," continues to undercut the emotional intensity of the opening. It leads the reader by a subtler method into the nature of Ichabod's failure, while the final word "fall" hints at the plight of the fallen angels.

In the following stanzas Ichabod is presented as the light of his age, a leader who has extinguished himself in the blackness of night. With the introduction of "night," the opposition of the two symbols, light and dark, is stated. The negation of the light is developed by a series of related terms—storm, night, and dark—which are expanded into more abstract words—passion, shame, dishonor, sadness, and death. The reader still is not certain what Ichabod's loss is, but it is definitely seen to be more than a fall from power or strength; a moral or intellectual loss is indicated. The fourth stanza opens with Ichabod's "bright" soul being driven from radiant hope by goading fiends. His position is now fully connected with the fallen angels and their sin of pride. The next stanzas present Whittier's response to Ichabod's spiritual death with the sense of loss and pity that a mourner would feel at a funeral. Whittier's plea for compassion moves the reader far more strongly than a rhetorical denunciation of the man. In the seventh stanza Ichabod is explicitly called a fallen angel who has sinned in pride of thought, thus fulfilling the suggestions of the earlier stanzas. The lines "naught/Save power remains" ironically heighten the worthlessness of the material power Ichabod sought, contrasting it to the now lost treasures of integrity and peace. The climax comes in the following stanza:

> All else is gone; from those great eyes
>   The soul has fled:
> When faith is lost, when honor dies,
>   The man is dead!

As one critic has pointed out, these lines echo Dante's horrible picture of the sinner whose soul was sent to hell before he actually died, leaving his body inhabited by demons. The last two lines reveal the true meaning of the light image—it is the symbol of wholesomeness and truth, the attunement of the soul to the guiding voice of the Holy Spirit. The final elegaic lines address the mourners, asking them to recall Ichabod's former greatness and to hide their personal sense of betrayal and loss. In this poem thought and imagery are interchangeable and are sustained with a dramatic intensity as indignation is tempered with pity.

◦◦◦

As this brief survey of over three hundred nature, personal, occasional, and antislavery poems indicates, only a score merit present-day reading and then barely four or five rise to the level of superior poetry. Whittier violates every canon of good artistry in these poems with his uninspired reworkings of trite ideas, repetitious tributes to personal friends, fondness for sentimentality and moralizing, and limited response to external beauty. It is here that the best case may be made for Whittier's failure as a poet, but it can be advanced only by neglecting his ballad and genre triumphs.

9

Hyatt waggoner has commented that Whittier's own age primarily read him as a religious poet and that he might be better understood and more widely appreciated if the modern age would consider him as such. Certainly there is much truth in that remark, for a strict moral code governed Whittier's writing and critical beliefs. In a sense most of his ballads, genre pieces, and nature poems are religious, since they so openly reflect his admiration for spiritual strength, his deep faith in the goodness of God, and his love of fellow man as a sharer in the divine essence. The antislavery writing of his middle years was completely based on a sense of moral injustice and it drew heavily on the Bible for illustrations and allusions. This intense spiritual consciousness permeated all aspects of his life and found a natural expression in religious lyrics and hymns. Especially in his later years when his Abolitionist work was over, Whittier searched poetically for the meaning of life and religion.

Few of these lyrics immortalize religious truths. Mainly they testify to the universality and moving simplicity of Whittier's Quaker faith and openly present his innermost beliefs, the ideals for which he fought and suffered. Sincerity and emotional feelings are tenuous, almost impossible, things to analyze; yet these qualities give Whittier's religious verses an unquestionable value and cont:nued popularity. In these poems are scores of references to defnite biblical passages and familiar biblical images. Even his technique imitated the psalmists' use of parallelism and repetition and their delight in reworking well-known themes. Though Whittier had a scholar's knowledge of the Bible, the Quaker interpretation of its humanitarian aspects rather than a more formalized application provided the main themes for his religious poetry. His absolute confidence in the goodness of God, his intense dislike of ritual, and his insistence that the everyday acts of brotherhood are the finest religious service were all sound Quaker doctrine and practice. Few writers of the nineteenth century felt more deeply or understood more profoundly the essential aspects of Christianity held by the Quakers. Poems such as "The Meeting," "First-Day Thoughts," "Andrew Rykman's Prayer," "Worship," and "The Shadow and the Light" provide an excellent introduction into the philosophy and ideas of the Friends. "The Meeting" contains a well-thought-out defense of the silent meetings. For, as Whittier explains, outward forms of worship, even nature herself, distract the senses and often hide God. Only in "the strength of mutual purpose" and from "the silence multiplied" can one truly hear the voice of God. If man is to obtain salvation, he and God must be in direct communication. "Worship" reveals Whittier's Quaker bias against music, incense, vestments, and sacrifice; yet its conclusion rises above a narrow sectarianism to reassert Whittier's one great message:

> O brother man! fold to thy heart thy brother;
> Where pity dwells, the peace of God is there;
> To worship rightly is to love each other,
> Each smile a hymn, each kindly deed a prayer.

"The Shadow and the Light" restates Whittier's confidence in the Inner Light and also illustrates his main failures with religious poetry: lack of condensation, poor organization, inability to visualize abstract thought, and awkward shifts in tone and emotion. This poem emphasizes man's needless doubts and fears which cause him to turn from God and neglect his mercy. As the title indicates, an underlying themal unity is developed by the contrast of the darkness and shadows of man's efforts against the light of God's truth. However, these images are repeated monotonously and without originality: man turns from the light, sets his face against the day, walks in shadows, wanders in unknown paths, refuses to look upon the light, and leaves the sun. In the midst of these repetitious images are sections of great lyric beauty:

> O Love Divine!—whose constant beam
> Shines on the eyes that will not see,
> And waits to bless us, while we dream.
>
> .　　.　　.　　.　　.　　.　　.
>
> O Beauty, old yet ever new!
> Eternal Voice, and Inward Word.

The widespread hymnal use of Whittier's religious lyrics indicates their worth as expressions of universal religious beliefs. Though few of his poems were written expressly for that purpose, Whittier is often regarded as the greatest American hymn writer. "The Eternal Goodness" is one of Whittier's most popular religious lyrics and perfectly fulfills the requirements for hymnal use. First of all, its theme of trust in God's love and mercy is an expression of the nineteenth century's religious optimism, which reasserted itself strongly in the face of growing scientific opposition to traditional Christian beliefs. When Whittier stated, "I know not of His hate,—I know/His goodness and His love," he was speaking for millions of Christians. Also the poem mirrored the widespread belief that God has a personal interest in man's salvation, unlike the angry God of Calvinistic dogma. Its clarity makes the poem perfectly understandable, and it contains no metaphysical complexities such as delighted the religious poets of the seventeenth century. Throughout, God's goodness is contrasted with worldly evil and sinfulness. Whittier admits that he cannot fathom the mind of God, but rebukes those who try to fix "mete and bound" to God's love, for God does not need the explanation of creed or logic.

The opening of the poem effectively matches Whittier's faltering, humble search for God against the confident audacity of the dogmatists. He walks the quiet aisles of prayer and his steps are hushed, while they "tread with boldness shod"; his hands are weak, while they hold iron creeds; and he looks for a plain robe, while they seek a king. This simple contrast is pointed and suggestive and permits Whittier to reveal his personal religious preferences without appearing didactic. Also the ballad form makes it read smoothly and allows easy memorizing. The movement of the following stanzas is direct and swift as it continues the contrast of the opening:

> I see the wrong that round me lies,
>   I feel the guilt within;
> I hear, with groan and travail-cries,
>   The world confess its sin.
>
> Yet, in the maddening maze of things,
>   And tossed by storm and flood,
> To one fixed trust my spirit clings;
>   I know that God is good!

The simple repetition of "I" heightens the intensity and force of the soul's search and leads to the final statement of truth. Also the emphasis on the word "know" throughout the middle section symbolizes the poet's complete emotional and mental acceptance, a knowing that transcends mere logic or material fact.

The emotional heart of the poem is delayed until the conclusion and then presented with a lyric beauty:

> And so beside the Silent Sea
>   I wait the muffled oar;
> No harm from Him can come to me
>   On ocean or on shore.
>
> I know not where His islands lift
>   Their fronded palms in air;
> I only know I cannot drift
>   Beyond His love and care.

Whittier's complete trust in God's love is concretely and effectively demonstrated by the imagery. The symbols are universal: the sea of death and the journey of the soul through the unknown toward a paradise of rest and palm trees. The tone is deliberately hushed by the connotations of "muffled," "drift," "fronded" and by the assonance of the o's, m's, and s's. The diction is close to ordinary speech with only eight dissyllables out of the nearly fifty words in these two stanzas. Structurally, "The Eternal Goodness" is typical of Whittier's religious poetry, since it is composed of individual stanzas of beautifully expressed ideas and images, all loosely connected by a general theme.

Like many of the longer psalms, "Our Master" is also a collection of separate verses grouped around a unifying theme. The poem represents and exalts Christ as the incarnation of immortal love. Whittier shows that Christ is not found in books, in creeds, in impressive cathedrals, or in heaven itself, but only in the heart and in the humanitarian practice of virtue. Sections of the poem are as good lyric poetry as Whittier ever wrote:

> Immortal Love, forever full,
>   Forever flowing free,
> Forever shared, forever whole,
>   A never-ebbing sea!
>
> .   .   .   .
>
> Blow, winds of God, awake and blow
>   The mists of earth away!
> Shine out, O Light Divine, and show
>   How wide and far we stray!
>
> Hush every lip, close every book,
>   The strife of tongues forbear;
> Why forward reach or backward look,
>   For love that clasps like air?
>
> We may not climb the heavenly steeps
>   To bring the Lord Christ down:
> In vain we search the lowest deeps,
>   For him no depths can drown.

The first stanza reproduces the flowing movement of the sea by using polysyllabic words, repetition, and alliteration and also expresses one of the divine mysteries of Christianity, the constancy of a God who gives all and yet is never lessened. The following three stanzas consider the omnipresence of God and man's vain attempts to find him in outward forms. Presenting the mystical side of Whittier's poetry, these lines suggest and examine some of the deeper implications of the Inner Light. The poet asks God to scatter the mists of earthly activities which obscure our spiritual goals, so we may be directed by the light of truth. Probingly, he questions those who only follow a historical Christ of set rules, who neglect Jesus' message for their own justification and narrow interpretation, and who fruitlessly wait for another physical Christ to appear. These people ignore God's knowledge and love which are as common as the air we breathe. Paradoxically, Christ is just as intangible as air to those who seek him in books or romantic daydreams. Considering this, Whittier remarks that we cannot hope to bring Christ down from heaven (by religious forms like the Eucharist) nor can we expect to find him in the lowest depths (by living a material life). The whole poem illuminates Whittier's Quaker belief in personal communication with God rather than reliance on authority and formal religion. This awareness of the indwelling reality of the Holy Spirit is the core of the Inner Light doctrine. It is an abstract and difficult concept—one which is doubly hard to express poetically. Herein lies the value of the lyric, for it does embody these abstractions clearly and imagistically.

◆§ §◆

Few of Whittier's religious poems sustain a high lyric intensity by turning on a single thought or by keeping one emotional note throughout. However, "Laus Deo," "The Brewing of Soma," and "At Last" fulfill these conditions. "Laus Deo" was occasioned by the ringing of Amesbury's town bells on the passage of the amendment abolishing slavery. Whittier said that the poem "wrote itself, or rather sang itself, while the bells rang." Certainly a heavy rhythmical beat and religious sense of exultation and emotional release are its outstanding characteristics. Catching the long and heavy peals of the bells with slight pauses in between strokes, the lines echo the bells:

> It is done!
> Clang of bell and roar of gun
> Send the tidings up and down.
> How the belfries rock and reel!
> How the great guns, peal on peal,
> Fling the joy from town to town!

With slight variations, this pattern continues throughout the whole poem as the boom of the bells sounds in the words of triumph and joy. The poem is a deeply personal, heartfelt expression of the pent-up emotions of over thirty years' work. The words Whittier chooses and their careful balance, such as "rock and reel," "loud and long," "ring and swing," add to the musical tone of the poem. Still, this exultation only re-echoes the poem's main theme— Whittier's humble awareness that God, not he, brought about the end of slavery. To emphasize this Whittier connects the booming sound of the bells with the Old Testament descriptions of the thundering voice of God when he spoke to his followers. The emotional intensity of the first two stanzas is relieved when the poet says "Let us kneel" to acknowledge his own unworthiness before God's awesome goodness. Then in two forceful stanzas, which paraphrase Miriam's song of triumph over the Egyptians, Whittier asserts the power and strength of God's action. As if dazed by the miracle that has taken place, Whittier softens his tone and presents his vision of the "fresher life" now made possible. In the final stanzas Whittier returns to the exultation of the opening and again imitates the psalms of triumph:

> Ring and swing,
> Bells of joy! On morning's wing
> Send the song of praise abroad!
> With a sound of broken chains
> Tell the nations that He reigns,
> Who alone is Lord and God!

The emotional variations in the poem range from intense happiness to awe and allow the fullest lyric development, pausing only to rise again on the crest of the poet's jubilation.

"The Brewing of Soma" combines two diverse themes, Whittier's Quaker dislike of formalized worship and his prayer for God's proper direction. Instead of stringing out various ideas on the two topics, Whittier blends the two sections into a unified whole. The opening survey of ritualistic excesses leads naturally into an ending plea for a return to the simplicity of early Christianity. The title, which becomes a symbol for all debased forms of worship, refers to an ancient practice of drinking alcohol brewed by priests to honor pagan gods. The poem opens with a realistic account of the brewing and the effects of "the drink of gods" upon the priests and people:

> They drank, and lo! in heart and brain
> A new, glad life began;
> The gray of hair grew young again,
> The sick man laughed away his pain,
> The cripple leaped and ran.

Whittier acknowledges that this was done in primitive ignorance, in a "child-world's early year"; yet scanning his own Christian era he sees all too clearly that sacrifices, rituals, and mysteries continue to "brew in many a Christian fane/The heathen Soma still!"

Then follows Whittier's most famous hymn, "Dear Lord and Father of Mankind," which begs God to forgive "our foolish ways" and pleads for a return to the "simple trust" of the first apostles. This shift from censure to petition is in the best psalmist tradition. From the harsh, objective description of the brewing the poet moves to a more personal view of similar trends in his own day; finally his soul speaks out, supplicating God to give his people the grace necessary for peace and true worship. The whole section turns on Whittier's concept of primitive Christianity where Christ's parables, miracles, and actual living of his gospel of love were the sources for religious expression. Also the section is studded with biblical references which suggest other examples of Christ's practice and give a tone of reverence to his plea. These six stanzas stress the words peace, rest, silence, simplicity, order, and coolness —the exact opposite of the turmoil, anxiety, noise, and fever of the earlier stanzas. The images and phrases preserve this tone of serenity as Christ's words come to us in a still, small voice; his breath is coolness; and his grace is noiseless like the falling of dew. The last stanza contrasts both methods of worshiping God with the peace and quiet of Christ rising above the "earthquake, wind, and fire." The poem expresses the simple, moving faith of a man whose love for Christ transcends creeds and rituals.

❧ ☙

"At Last," written in 1882, is the culmination of Whittier's poetic search for the assurance of personal immortality. In the poem Whittier pleads for God's mercy to obtain a heaven which corresponds to his earthly home and which contains all his departed loved ones. The poem opens with a tone of mystery and strangeness:

> When on my day of life the night is falling,
>   And, in the winds from unsunned spaces blown,
> I hear far voices out of darkness calling
>   My feet to paths unknown.

The next two stanzas intensify this fear and uncertainty as the soul recalls how pleasant its "home of life" was; and then realizes that all the familiar things of life, "earth, sky, home's pictures," are fading. Only God can help and the soul cries to him, "I have but Thee, my Father." Repeating this petition and stressing his own unworthiness, the poet carefully reworks the opening images, as the "voices out of darkness" become familiar faces and hymns of joy and the "paths unknown" turn to sheltering restful homes by peaceful rivers. Whittier's unsophisticated view of heaven completes the poem:

> No gate of pearl, no branch of palm I merit,
>   Nor street of shining gold.
>
> .   .   .   .
>
> Some humble door among Thy many mansions,
>   Some sheltering shade where sin and striving cease,
> And flows forever through heaven's green expansions
>   The river of Thy peace.

❦ ❧

In general, Whittier's religious lyrics fail to match his best ballads and genre pieces. Most of them do not sustain a true lyric note and are marred by repetitious thought and commonplace imagery. Yet here his penchant for didacticism is no handicap; and the easily grasped meaning, universal themes, effective imagery, and religious sincerity of particular poems fulfill all the qualifications for good hymns. The style of these poems is artless and direct; the content is the philosophy that Whittier lived and fought for all his life. Though his religious poetry is not of the high order of Milton or Herbert, it conveys his hunger for practical moral action and confidence in God as "Our Father."

10

꧁ THE PROSE AND
MARGARET SMITH'S JOURNAL

ALTHOUGH Whittier's collected prose works come to over three
volumes, they have received only passing attention. The
scholar and historian have read them mainly for the information
and insight they furnish about Whittier's life and New England
legends. Certainly the bulk of his prose has little intrinsic value
or enduring literary merit. As a historical document *Justice and
Expediency* still repays reading for its fervid yet logical presentation of the basic Abolitionist position. Arguing from economic and
political premises as well as moral ones, Whittier highlights slavery's disastrous effects on competitive labor and the democratic
rights of free speech and press. He draws heavily from Burke and
Milton for his ideas on the validity of justice over expediency and
even employs their manner of expression.

For the modern reader, Whittier's regional prose essays, written
in the 1840's, are the most interesting and appealing. "Charms
and Fairy Faith" and " Magicians and Witch Folk" deal with old
superstitions, sorceresses, and folk legends and are filled with
local touches that echo the ballads and genre poems. The more
whimsical and nostalgic "Pope Night," "The Great Ipswich
Fright," and "The Fish I Didn't Catch" present Whittier's per-

sonal recollections of boyhood excitement and delight in rural traditions and tall tales. "Yankee Gypsies" is typical of these sketches, as Whittier describes in a loose, wandering manner a host of vagrants, tramps, and itinerant preachers who had traveled from farmhouse to farmhouse in search of work or alms. These peddlers and beggars were a familiar sight in Whittier's youth and he depicts them with surety and ease, making them live and claim interest. The picturesque details and caricatures give a charm to many sections, such as the following:

> One—I think I see him now, grim, gaunt, and ghastly, working his slow way up to our door—used to gather herbs by the wayside and call himself doctor. He was bearded like a he goat and used to counterfeit lameness, yet, when he supposed himself alone, would travel on lustily as if walking for a wager . . . Another used to go stooping, like Bunyan's pilgrim, under a pack made of an old bed-sacking, stuffed out into most plethoric dimensions, tottering on a pair of small, meagre legs, and peering out with his wild, hairy face from under his burden like a big-bodied spider. . . . [Another] brought with him pins, needles, tape, and cotton thread for my mother; jack-knives, razors, and soap for my father; and verses of his own composing, coarsely printed and illustrated with rude wood-cuts, for the delectation of the younger branches of the family. No lovesick youth could drown himself, no deserted maiden bewail the moon, no rogue mount the gallows, without fitting memorial in [his] verses. Earthquakes, fires, fevers, and shipwrecks he regarded as personal favors from Providence, furnishing the raw material of song and ballad.

❧ ❧

Whittier's longest and most important piece of prose, *Margaret Smith's Journal in the Province of Massachusetts Bay, 1678–9,* is a surprising achievement in light of these other careless sketches. Though suffused with Whittier's humanitarian philosophy and personal interest in Quakerism, slavery, and witchcraft, it is a remarkably alive and accurate portrait of the Puritan theocracy in the 1670's. Most critics have duly commented on Whittier's skill in weaving various strands of old Colonial diaries, journals, and biographies into a believable historical fiction, but few have sensed the true function of Whittier's formal artistry in creating literary value for the theme and imparting significance to the historical materials. Yet in the *Journal* Whittier's choice and knowledge of the journal genre, his expansion and additions to dry fact, and his varied stylistic effects are fused with a sensitive insight into Puritan psychology to vividly portray the New England colonies of the time.

The framework and form of the piece harmonize perfectly with its theme and intended mood. It purports to be the journal kept by an English girl, Margaret Smith, as she visits the colonies from May, 1678 to June, 1679. Even the date is carefully selected to allow an objective handling of the Quaker-victimizing persecutions and witchcraft terror and to prevent Margaret from being emotionally involved in contemporary disputes. So she only hears of the Quaker trials in the 1650's and then the events are recounted by an aged servant of Endicott who sympathizes with the Puritan side. The looseness of the journal form, a casual day-to-day record of Margaret's travels, and her position as a niece of the influential Edward Rawson gave Whittier complete freedom to comment on religious and political issues, to depict major historical figures, and to describe picturesquely the surrounding countryside. Also Margaret's travels in Maine and Rhode Island present her with fresh, impartial views of the Puritan state. As a result she notes with relief that Maine inhabitants can throw off the "sober and grave" manner of the Puritans and even defy Massachusetts' court authority. The religious harmony among the different sects in Rhode Island amazes her after experiencing the dogmatism and intolerance of the Bay Colony Puritans. To avoid the usual pitfalls of the Puritan journals with their often monotonous soul searching and sectarian interests, Whittier purposefully chose a young girl for narrator. As Margaret Smith says, she wrote for "the partial eye of my kinsman" and not for "the critical observance of the scholar." Following her own impulsive interests, she is curious about the baking of native bread, notes the attire of Indian girls, records with wry humor her censure for being immodest in wearing stylish dresses, and even observes how dun fish is cured on the Isles of Shoals. Who else but a woman on ordination day in zealous New England would dare bypass its inner spiritual significance to comment:

> It was quite a sight the next morning to see the people coming in from the neighboring towns, and to note their odd dresses, which were indeed of all kinds, from silks and velvets to coarsest homespun woolens, dyed with hemlock, or oil-nut bark, and fitting so ill

that, if they had all cast their clothes into a heap, and then each snatched up whatsoever coat or gown came to hand, they could not have suited worse.

As an inquisitive visitor she would be expected to observe more closely the colors of the woods in the fall, the effects of the summer's heat on the grass, the dreary coldness of winter rains, and the lavish display of spring flowers, and to be objective and tolerant about local prejudices. Finally her youth and sympathetic nature allow her to play a major role in the love plot as confidant for Rebecca Rawson in her infatuation for Sir Thomas Hale and as an interested observer of her brother's love for Margaret Brewster.

Even with these additions to the scope of the *Journal,* Whittier remained artistically true to the spirit and distinctiveness of the Puritan mind. Drawing on his extensive readings in Colonial diaries, histories, biographies, and family records, Whittier has Margaret describe many characteristic incidents of the "wonderworking Providence of Zion's Savior." At the very opening of the *Journal* she praises God for her safe voyage, later recognizes the homecoming of a soldier long supposed dead as a "strange and wonderful providence," and dutifully records God's punishments for a man who hid a papist gold cross. Throughout the *Journal* she piously moralizes on changes in climate, acts of friendship, and learned sermons. For further authenticity Whittier inserted typical incidents from the journals and histories of Sewall, Knight, Mather, and Johnson. For example, Samuel Sewall's diary for July 8, 1677, records: "In sermon time there came in a female Quaker, in a Canvas frock, her hair dishevelled and loose like a Periwigg, her face as black as ink, led by two other Quakers, and two other[s] followed. It occasioned the greatest and most amazing uproar that I ever saw." Correspondingly, in Whittier's *Journal* this entry occurs for July 6th: "Yesterday a strange thing happened in the meetinghouse. ... A young woman, barefooted, and with a coarse canvas frock about her, and her long hair hanging loose like a periwig, and sprinkled with ashes, came walking up the south aisle." In another section Whittier uses Cotton Mather's account of the haunted Morse house found in the *Magnalia Christi Americana.* Instead of Mather's wearisome listing of unbelievable detail and cataloguing of supposed witchcraft signs, Whittier selects a few appropriate details such as tools flying about the room, baskets dropping down the chimney, and hearth irons dancing, to effectively satirize the delusion and then dramatizes a typical incident when Margaret is present. Again the humorous description which Margaret gives of the aged Deacon Dole, a widower of three years, in his unsuccessful courting of Dame Prudence parallels the unintentional humor of Sewall's wooing of Mrs. Denison and Mrs. Winthrop. Also Margaret's account of her travels to Rhode Island closely resembles the conversational tone, rich idiom, and graphic art of Sarah Kemble Knight's journal. Like Madame Knight, Margaret has her trouble with high uncomfortable beds, unpalatable food, and crude and carping innkeepers, and even meets with some frenzied Quakers whose singing and ranting repel her.

Originally Whittier's *Journal* employed all the external mannerisms of seventeenth-century writing, the capitalization of nouns, use of italics, substitution of "ie" for "y," and added letters. Though these stylistic devices were regularized in the final edition, his presentation still conveys a feeling of remoteness and the atmosphere of past Colonial times:

> The weather suddenly changing from a warm rain and mist to sharp, clear cold, the trees a little way from the house did last evening so shine with a wonderful brightness in the light of the moon, now nigh unto its full, that I was fain to go out upon the hill-top to admire them. And truly it was no mean sight to behold every small twig becrusted with ice, and glittering famously like silverwork or crystal, as the rays of the moon did strike upon them. Moreover, the earth was covered with frozen snow, smooth and hard like to marble . . . bedight with frost . . . hemlocks, pines, and spruces, starred and bespangled, as if wetted with a great rain of molten crystal.

Here the use of archaic terms such as "now nigh," "I was fain," and "bedight," along with the excessive predication shows a conscious imitation of the Colonial idiom. As in the best Puritan writing the phrases and images are direct and original, bypassing classical allusions for plain native figures. Though the short and irregular rhythm of the passage lacks the sweeping rise and fall of rhetorical balance, there is a natural awareness of sound (as the "s" emphasis near the end of the passage) which prevents its being uninteresting. Throughout the *Journal* similar stylistic devices are consistently well-used and do establish a definite feeling of former days. Also Margaret's sprightly and worldly descriptions

John G. Whittier

enliven what would typically be an intense account of a soul's search for God. She and Rebecca mock a learned minister for censuring their fashionable dresses, quote witty, light verse, and plot to send "all the sour, crabbed, busybodies in the churches, off to Rhode Island, where . . . one crazy head could not reproach another."

One innovation added by Whittier to the *Journal* framework was a love plot centering on the disastrous romance of Rebecca Rawson and Thomas Hale and the happy marriage of Leonard Smith to Margaret Brewster. Since Whittier fails to develop character motivation and often neglects the love affairs for long digressions, their plausibility and dramatic interest are minimized, and this element remains the weakest part of the *Journal*. One never understands why Rebecca accepts Thomas Hale rather than the honest, plain spoken Robert Pike, and she only remarks: "When I am with him [Pike], I sometimes wish I had never seen Sir Thomas. But my choice is made." Nor is Leonard's sudden marriage to the Quaker girl Margaret Brewster anything more than a narrative device to permit further comment on Quaker life and the persecutions. Also Whittier intersperses throughout the *Journal* numerous unrelated tales of miraculously reunited lovers, a tormented Jesuit knight, and sudden Indian friendships in the midst of battle—all of which expose the thinness of the plot. The fondness for melodrama and sentimentality in these tales echoes the popular taste of the nineteenth century rather than the sterner, more disciplined world of Colonial New England. On the whole, the plot most clearly demonstrates that Whittier's talent was not original or inventive, for his presentation is surest when utilizing historical or legendary sources rather than relying on his own imagination.

Much happier than this ill-adapted plot is Whittier's presentation of the conversations and sermons of the leading Colonial divines. All types are delineated: the intolerant, sternly just ministers like Wilson and Ward; the pompous, self-righteous figures like Norton and Richardson; and the simple, sincere men of God like Eliot and Dr. Russ. The heart of the *Journal's* theme, a plea for love and toleration in dissension-tossed New England, is found in a sermon by Dr. Russ. Following the rhetorical pattern of Puritan discourse, it opens with an appropriate quotation from Scripture, explicates the meaning of the passage, and then applies the lesson to the general Colonial situation. Expounding on "Char-

ity seeketh not her own," Russ illustrates the force of mutual
benevolence and the failure of self-love in obtaining happiness.

> But he that hath found charity to be the temper of happiness. . . .
> hath discovered a more subtle alchemy than any of which the phi-
> losophers did dream,—for he transmuteth the enjoyment of others
> into his own, and his large and open heart partaketh of the satis-
> faction of all around him. Are there any here who, in the midst of
> outward abundance, are sorrowful of heart,—who go mourning . . .
> who long for serenity of spirit . . . Let such seek out the poor and
> forsaken. . . . In love and compassion, God hath made us de-
> pendent upon each other.

The careful balancing and expansion of ideas in the series of "who"
clauses and pairing of nouns, the climaxing of rhetorical questions
with the final serene assurance of "love and compassion," and the
concentration on thought rather than image (the only real figure
is the well-worn one from alchemy) are in perfect accord with
the better Colonial sermons where presentation emphasizes the
logic of the discourse.

Dramatically, this key sermon is framed by Mr. Richardson's
talk of the previous day, which demands hate and vengeance instead of charity and tolerance. Richardson sensationalizes popular
superstitions about witchcraft into dramatic proofs of the devil's
activities and prays that the revelation of those "who have made
a covenant with hell" will gain glory for the New England saints.
Later on another minister, John Norton, presents a further contrast to the piety and humility of Dr. Russ when he justifies the
recent hanging of a Quaker woman by cautioning against pity and
tolerance:

> The death of these poor bodies is a bitter thing, but the death of
> the soul is far more dreadful; and it is better that these people
> should suffer than that hundreds of precious souls should be lost
> through their evil communication. The care of the dear souls of
> my flock lieth heavily upon me, as many sleepless nights and days
> of fasting do bear witness. I have not taken counsel of flesh and
> blood in this grave matter, nor yielded unto the natural weakness
> of my heart. And while some were for sparing these workers of
> iniquity, even as Saul spared Agag, I have been strengthened, as
> it were, to hew them in pieces before the Lord in Gilgal.

Though harsh, Norton's speech represents a definite and understandable Puritan position, but his bigoted manner of presenting

his opinions is particularly repugnant. No one is allowed to forget his self-righteous fasting and inner sorrow about these victims, nor his chosen position as the agent of God ("a watchman on the walls of Zion" as he puts it). The very pattern of the speech with its awkward interruptions and pedantic biblical allusions creates an unpleasant, stilted tone.

Decorating his work with these more formal devices, Whittier erected a solid Colonial dwelling and peopled it with lively figures who realistically grappled with the important issues of the day. In characterization as in plot Whittier was not overly successful, but here the essential traits of the Puritan are delineated with a surprising closeness to modern interpretation. The chief merit of his portrayal is its awareness of the inner tensions of duty and emotions in the Puritan nature and its accurate, unbiased presentation of them. Whittier sympathized with their efforts to cultivate an unyielding rocky soil, admired their devotion to learning and education, and understood their determination to establish a "new Canaan" in the Bay Colony. Constantly Whittier humanizes the Puritans: Mr. Ward's bigotry and intolerance are balanced by his delight in practical jokes and light verse. Cotton Mather's pretensions and dogmatism are softened by his youth and earnestness. A dying Puritan soldier forgives the Indians who wounded him, finally understanding the Indians' just grievance against the white invaders. Robert Pike represents the finest product of the Puritan culture with his refusal to be swayed by local prejudices, his acceptance of pain and hardship, his instinctive gentility which is uncoarsened by a farmer's life, and his knowledge and love of nature. Edward Rawson, who was long secretary of the colony, exemplifies Whittier's approach. Rawson is shown as a practical, outspoken man whose harshness and severity are mollified by common sense and humanity. Completely loyal to the Puritan theocracy, he still wonders if strict laws and drastic punishments are the best method for curing dissenters. Since the Bible and his ministers insist upon the reality of witchcraft, he can believe in it and he is willing to see those justly accused tried and hanged. Yet characteristically he tries to obtain reprieves for the accused and scoffs at the attempts to brand women witches because they are senile or surly. When he meets a drunken Indian, loudly plotting revenge on his white master, Rawson sends the man off to bed rather than to the stocks. He speaks out strongly for liberty and the rights of self-rule, and then notes bitterly that the colonists fail to turn out on voting day. Even his condemnation of the Quakers and other dissenters springs from a sense of duty, rather than morbidness or inner anxiety. Only one outburst reveals the repressed tensions of his harsh existence. When Margaret Smith tells him that her brother is going to marry a Quakeress, he wrathfully asks if she were going "to turn Quaker, and fall to prophesying," and then promises a whipping for her brother "if he come hither a *theeing* and *thouing* of me." Yet later on he allows Margaret to visit her brother in Rhode Island. Ironically, common sense fails to guide his actions only in Rebecca's marriage, for he allows his daughter to reject the more suitable Robert Pike for the gallant Thomas Hale in the hopes that she might achieve nobility.

Other characters, especially the ministers, reveal less pleasing aspects of the Puritan mind by their dogmatic insistence on the Bible as the complete guide for every phase of manners and social relationships. Margaret is hardly in Boston a day when she is warned against wearing lace ruffles and long sleeves, and later she is criticized for "immodest laying out of the hair." A humorous comment on the lack of good poetry in the Cambridge Psalm Book evokes Mr. Richardson's heated remarks that "it is not seemly to jest over the Word of God . . . God's altar needs no polishing." When hard-pressed in an argument about the validity of holding slaves, another minister nicely makes a distinction between slaves captured in the war and those taken in peacetime. More definitely Whittier flays the hatred and persecutions suffered by the Quakers, but does not, though one might expect it, become an apologist for the sect. He shows the Quakers' courage, dignity, and piety, while also severely criticizing them for their excesses: the frenzied singing and ranting, wild prophesying, and outlandish demands for the destruction of government. On her visit to Rhode Island Margaret comments that the traditional Quaker gravity and staid deportment ill-accord with her natural spirits. Especially she criticizes "the more simple and unlearned, [who] affect a painful and melancholy look and a canting tone of discourse." Even "the dark and haughty Endicott," whose bitter hatred of the Quakers is thwarted in the poem "Cassandra Southwick," is humanized as we see him pulling hard at his long tuft of hair when displeased, wearing mended velvet breeches, and honestly trying to keep peace in his land by driving the Quakers out. Throughout his account of the Quakers and their trials Whittier's objectivity and impartiality add depth to the historical accuracy.

One of the most intriguing topics handled in the *Journal* is the witchcraft belief of the average colonist. Whittier was most familiar with the pattern of local superstitions and understood how the credulous and excitement-starved nature of rural people would feed upon these tales. The ministers themselves are held to be the most responsible for the hysteria by their misguided insistence on the reality of witches and their unrestrained sermons on the power of the devil's efforts to corrupt their Bible state. In the *Journal* Whittier traces the course of a witchcraft delusion which begins with the mischievous pranks devised by Goody Morse's son to frighten his parents. Gradually the populace accepts the strange noises, mysterious disappearance of kitchen utensils, and the sight of flying wood as supernatural, and eventually demands that Goody Morse be hanged as a witch. Whittier ridicules the validity of the spectral evidence presented against her by noting that the court had accused her of afflicting the child of Widow Goodwin and of flying about in the sun "as if she had been cut in twain, or as if the devil did hide the lower part of her." Robert Pike justly remarks of such evidence that "it ought not to hang a cat." Both Pike and Dr. Russ sense that the real causes of the witchcraft scare lay in the morbid zeal of the accusers, their thwarted personalities, and their avid desire for excitement; but these two are not always able to stem the tide of ignorance and hysteria. Indeed, they themselves are suspect for their enlightened views; and, for using reason rather than imagination in examining the supposed witchcraft cases, they are denounced as adherents of the devil. The accused witches, Goody Cole and Goody Morse, are depicted as querulous, even senile, women who deserve pity, not hanging; and their accusers act from ignorance or are motivated by "witch hunters" like the repulsive Goody Marston, who "scrupled not to say that she would as lief stick an Indian as a hog, and who walked all the way from Marblehead to Boston to see the Quaker woman hung, and did foully jest over her dead body." Finally, when Margaret views the possessed children, she notes that one of them is vicious and spoiled and agrees with Robert Pike that the best cure for the child is a birch twig, smartly laid on. Here Whittier cuts directly to the core of the witchcraft dilemma by placing responsibility where it ought to be—on perverse and attention-seeking human nature—and most modern examinations of the problem have concurred with his analysis.

One other major theme in the *Journal* is the condemnation of the unjust and pitiless treatment of the few remaining Indians in the settled parts of the colonies. A shocked Margaret Smith records their isolation and extreme poverty, the filthy hovels in which they live, and their slave position under the white masters. The pathos and tragedy of the lost Indian heritage is seen in the return of an old Indian, Umpachee, to the ancient burial ground of his ancestors—now the farmland of Leonard Smith. Though impressed and moved by Leonard's kind treatment and his devout practice of Christianity, Umpachee refuses to leave the customs and worship of his tribal gods to adopt a new religion, for he fears that such an act might deny him a reunion with his tribe in an afterlife. Even Simon, an old drunken Indian reprobate, has his moments of dignity. He defends his poaching with the remark: "This all Indian Land. The Great Spirit made it for Indians. . . . He made land for White men too; but they left it and took Indian's land, because it was better." And then, when accused of drinking too much, he bitterly asks: "Who makes strong drink . . . Who takes the Indian's beaver-skins and corn for it?" Yet Whittier also criticizes the Indians for their failure to adjust to new circumstances and for their imitation of the white man's vices. Whittier's plea for mercy and sympathy for the Indian asserts the main theme of the *Journal,* the need for love and understanding among all people.

These selected examples illustrate how Whittier could vary the journal genre, expand his historical material, and capture stylistic differences to suit semidramatic occasions, different characters, and the theme itself. Here, as in few other fictional pieces, Whittier emotionally and imaginatively grasped his subject matter and presented it with ease and surety. Though all the chief tenets of his life—his love of old New England, hatred of intolerance, deep spirituality, and knowledge of local customs—are included in the *Journal,* they are united and subordinated to the whole picture of Colonial times. Thus, form and theme fuse to create his one prose success.

11

✒ ACHIEVEMENT

N EAR THE end of his life, Whittier characterized his work by
remarking: "I am not one of the master singers & don't
pose as one. By the grace of God I am only what I am, and don't
wish to pass for more." No one would deny the truth of his first
statement, but, almost perversely, critics have refused to consider
the implications of the second. Nineteenth-century writers over-
praised Whittier by mistakenly equating popular approval with
literary merit, while modern critics have employed this same popularity to gauge his artistic failure. Even the most sympathetic
biographers have slighted the poet to dwell on the fiery Abolitionist, the practical politician, and the religious humanist. In a casual
critical aside his official biographer noted that Whittier's verse
was "written first of all for the neighbors" and this remark illuminates the essence of Whittier's achievement. He did preserve what
was most particularly *his* and the neighbors'—*his* Quaker heritage, *his* Haverhill boyhood, *his* Merrimack scenery, *his* love of
local superstitions and legend, and *his* interest in Colonial times.
Unlike most of the genteel writers of the late nineteenth century,
Whittier was reared in a nonconformist Quaker faith; Burns's
homespun verses were his inspiration, not classical models; poverty, hard farmwork, and rural isolation educated him, rather
than college and travel. Until his fiftieth year Whittier remained

a despised Abolitionist, a radical propagandist poet, and a part-time editor who completely lacked the public approval and popular success of a Longfellow or Lowell. He was an anomalous figure among the accepted poets of the time, for he alone drew upon his native roots for inspiration. His meager formal education, social insularity, and parochial outlook made him a truly American product in a culture that was mainly derivative and based on English standards. His active life as a reformer and politician strengthened his tenacious hold on the basic realities of nature, family, and religion and nurtured his passionate devotion to the principles of liberty and tolerance. Through study and reading Whittier steeped his mind in the history and traditions of New England until he understood the past as he had experienced the present. Whittier's themes were few and limited, lacking the depth and social insight of the more cultured Holmes and Lowell. However, these topics of freedom, ethical action, and domestic emotion were his by years of practical experience and their constant reworking often burned away artistic impurities to leave a finely tempered product.

If Whittier had done no more than preserve New England traditions, reflect popular religious feeling and family emotions, and serve as the antislavery poet, he would merit a definite place in American cultural and social history. Yet an honest examination of his poetry indicates a much more enduring literary claim. Like all the genteel poets Whittier suffered from the diffusion and sentimentality inherent in the tradition of public rhetoric and he even lacked Longfellow's technical control and polish. Perhaps no other established nineteenth-century poet wrote so much poor verse, but the miracle is that by the most exacting poetic standards Whittier's best remains so good. Part of the credit must go to Whittier's Quaker training which emphasized simplicity and directness and which taught him an unusual appreciation of the beauty of the commonplace. Also Burns's native poetry reemphasized his Quaker belief in the value of personal response and made him realize that the familiar, often forgotten incidents of his own experience, such as a girl raking hay, beehives draped in black, the languor of a sultry summer day, were true poetic materials. To present these experiences Whittier gradually learned to render the natural setting with concrete, graphic pictures that accentuated salient local features; to create an atmosphere through unpolished country phrases, using the everyday language of the Haverhill and Merrimack farmer; and to achieve naturalness with the native imagery and simple techniques of the ballad form or with the rough pairings and halting movement of the rhymed octosyllabic line. Whittier's technique was old-fashioned, but this adequately fitted his rustic material and often deepened its impression.

Whittier's ballads and genre poems exemplify his critical beliefs and poetic practice. As a pioneer regionalist Whittier took moments of New England history and legend and fashioned them into realistic, exciting narrative. Of course, Whittier's poems are not imbued with the symbolic richness and psychological insight of Hawthorne's Colonial tales, but they capture old New England simply and pictorially as in a series of Flemish still lifes. (His particular skill in re-creating the past is seen most fully in "The Pennsylvania Pilgrim" and in his one long prose effort, *Margaret Smith's Journal*). Whittier instinctively responded to folk tales and could fit an acount of a skipper who had betrayed his own townspeople or the story of a woman who alone had defied rebel soldiers to the ballad requirements of emotionally filled dialogue, sparse imagery, and concentrated action. At his best Whittier expanded the simple narrative appeal of these tales by dramatic development and psychological insight.

Similarly Whittier's genre, nature, and occasional poems elevated the ordinary details of Essex County life into a universal expression of boyhood innocence, romantic dreams, and agrarian simplicity, which not only recorded social history but caught the pathos of a dying rural tradition. If Whittier idealized and typified the barefoot boy days, the district school days, and the harvest-filled autumn days, he also perceived the flaws of romantic love and sentimental idealism. In his rustic anecdotes of local eccentrics, in his humorous but respectful portraits of unyielding, practical New Englanders, in his introspective examinations of moral tensions, and in his indignation at injustice, Whittier captured the essence of the Puritan mind. His selected use of local scenery and picturesque detail blend with his laconic native humor to add depth and vividness to his genre and nature poems. In these poems Whittier stands midway in the direct line of American poetic expression that stretches from Anne Bradstreet to Robert Frost.

Perhaps Walt Whitman best summed up Whittier's religious

poetry when he said that Whittier shows "the zeal, the moral energy that founded New England" and that his poetry "stands for morality . . . as filter'd through the positive Puritanical and Quaker filters; [it] is very valuable as a genuine utterance." These qualities illuminate Whittier's religious lyrics and, despite their overelaboration and diffusiveness, these poems strikingly attest to the power of Christ's message of love and brotherhood. Whittier's intense response to the highest ideals of humanity and his sincere expression of practical Christianity have enshrined his religious verses among the finest expressions of American Protestant thought.

Possibly forty of Whittier's poems are still readable today and only a bare dozen stand out as superior. Though small, this output cannot be dismissed as insignificant. The blend of grotesque humor and tortured remorse in "Skipper Ireson's Ride," the exaggerated terror and the awesome, yet human, figure of the simple man who does his duty in "Abraham Davenport," the emotionally charged dilemma of a pacifist poet who longs to fight in "The Waiting," the ironic contrasts of the dream and reality woven throughout "Maud Muller," the symbolic development of a light–dark contrast to depict a lost soul in "Ichabod," the emotional variations achieved through the rhythm of ringing bells in "Laus Deo," and the skillful handling of repetition and childlike detail to mask the disturbing reality of nature's destruction in "Telling the Bees"—all these poems and others demonstrate Whittier's artistic ability and intrinsic literary achievement. Although Whittier's poems fall short of the poetic richness and imaginative depth of the major nineteenth-century poets such as Whitman, Dickinson, Poe, and Emerson, his verses exhibit more spiritual illumination and downright "grit" than the poems of Bryant, Longfellow, Lanier, and the other minor poets. His one sustained triumph, "Snow-Bound," remains the minor masterpiece of nineteenth-century poetry. Here Whittier's simple expression of the value of family affections and nostalgic longing for a past social order was deepened by his selected handling of concrete detail and by the symbolic development of the fire–storm contrast into an imperishable portrait of nineteenth-century rural American life.

Although definitely a minor poet, Whittier's place in American literature seems more secure than modern critics are willing to grant. He will continue to be read and enjoyed as long as people respond to their traditions and heritage and want to find honest expression of their fundamental democratic and religious feelings. Winfield Townley Scott's penetrating and whimsical poem "Mr. Whittier" aptly characterizes the man and illuminates the lasting quality of Whittier's achievement:

> It is easier to leave *Snow-Bound* and a dozen other items in or out of
> The school curriculum than it is to have written them. Try it and see.
>
> .   .   .   .
>
> It is so much easier to forget than to have been Mr. Whittier.
> He put the names of our places into his poems and he honored us with himself;
> And is for us but not altogether, because larger than us.

SELECTED BIBLIOGRAPHY

WHITTIER'S CHIEF WORKS

Legends of New England. Hartford: Hanmer and Phelps, 1831.
Justice and Expediency. Haverhill, Mass.: C. P. Thayer, 1833.
Poems. Philadelphia: Joseph Healy, 1838.
Lays of My Home, and Other Poems. Boston: W. D. Ticknor, 1843.
Voices of Freedom. Philadelphia: T. S. Cavender, 1846.
Leaves From Margaret Smith's Journal. Boston: Ticknor, Reed, and Fields, 1849.
Songs of Labor, and Other Poems. Boston: Ticknor, Reed, and Fields, 1850.
Home Ballads and Poems. Boston: Ticknor and Fields, 1860.
In War Time, and Other Poems. Boston: Ticknor and Fields, 1864.
Snow-Bound. Boston: Ticknor and Fields, 1866.
The Tent on the Beach, and Other Poems. Boston: Ticknor and Fields, 1867.
The Pennsylvania Pilgrim, and Other Poems. Boston: J. R. Osgood, 1872.
The Vision of Echard, and Other Poems. Boston: Houghton, Osgood, 1878.
The King's Missive, and Other Poems. Boston: Houghton Mifflin, 1881.
The Bay of Seven Islands, and Other Poems. Boston: Houghton Mifflin, 1883.

ADDITIONAL WORKS

A Study of Whittier's Apprenticeship as a Poet: Dealing with Poems Written between 1825 and 1835 not Available in the Poet's Collected Works by Francis Mary Pray. Bristol, N. H.: Musgrove Printing House, 1930.
Whittier on Writers and Writing: The uncollected critical writings of John Greenleaf Whittier, eds. Edwin Harrison Cady and Harry Hayden Clark. Syracuse: Syracuse University Press, 1950.

LETTERS

Life and Letters of John Greenleaf Whittier, ed. Samuel T. Pickard. 2 vols. Boston: Houghton Mifflin, 1894. [The main source for Whittier's letters.]
Whittier as a Politician, Illustrated by His Letters to Professor Elizur Wright, Jr., now first published, ed. Samuel T. Pickard. Boston: Charles E. Goodspeed, 1900.
Whittier Correspondence from the Oak Knoll Collection, ed. John Albree. Salem: Essex Book and Print Club, 1911.
Whittier's Unknown Romance, ed. Marie V. Denervaud. Boston: Houghton Mifflin, 1922.
Elizabeth Lloyd and the Whittiers. A Budget of Letters, ed. Thomas Franklin Currier. Cambridge: Harvard University Press, 1939.

COLLECTED WORKS

The Writings of John Greenleaf Whittier. 7 vols. Boston: Houghton Mifflin, 1888–1889. (Riverside Edition)

The Complete Poetical Works of John Greenleaf Whittier, ed. Horace E. Scudder. Boston and New York: Houghton Mifflin, 1894. (Cambridge Edition)

[There is a recent paperbound selection of Whittier's poems, edited by Donald Hall in the Dell Laurel Poetry Series.]

BIBLIOGRAPHY

Currier, Thomas Franklin. *A Bibliography of John Greenleaf Whittier.* Cambridge: Harvard University Press, 1937. [The complete, indispensable guide to Whittier bibliography up to 1937.]

Spiller, Robert E. et al. *Literary History of the United States,* Vol. III, *Bibliography.* New York: Macmillan, 1948. *Supplement,* ed. Richard M. Ludwig. New York: Macmillan, 1959.

BIOGRAPHY

Written by Relatives and Associates

Claflin, Mrs. Mary B. *Personal Recollections of John G. Whittier.* New York: Thomas Crowell, 1893.

Fields, Mrs. James T. *Whittier, Notes of His Life and Friendships.* New York: Harper, 1893.

Kennedy, William Sloane. *John G. Whittier, The Poet of Freedom.* New York: Funk & Wagnalls, 1892.

Pickard, Samuel T. *Life and Letters of John Greenleaf Whittier.* 2 vols. Boston: Houghton Mifflin, 1894. [The authorized biography and still the primary source book.]

Underwood, Francis H. *John Greenleaf Whittier; a Biography.* Boston: J. R. Osgood, 1884.

Written by Later Authors

Bennett, Whitman. *Whittier, Bard of Freedom.* Chapel Hill: University of North Carolina Press, 1941. [Most readable.]

Perry, Bliss. *John Greenleaf Whittier; a Sketch of His Life, with Selected Poems.* Boston: Houghton Mifflin, 1907.

Pollard, John A. *John Greenleaf Whittier, Friend of Man.* Boston: Houghton Mifflin, 1949. [Probably the definitive account of Whittier's life, though it completely neglects the poet.]

CRITICAL AND INTERPRETATIVE STUDIES FRAMED AS BIOGRAPHIES

Carpenter, George Rice. *John Greenleaf Whittier.* Boston: Houghton Mifflin, 1903. (American Men of Letters Series) [Still the best account of the man and poet.]

Higginson, Thomas Wentworth. *John Greenleaf Whittier.* New York: Macmillan, 1902. (English Men of Letters Series)

Mordell, Albert. *Quaker Militant: John Greenleaf Whittier.* Boston: Houghton Mifflin, 1933. [Highly partisan and slanted by a Freudian interpretation.]

SPECIALIZED STUDIES

Eastburn, Iola Kay. *Whittier's Relation to German Life and Thought.* Philadelphia: University of Pennsylvania Press, 1915.

Pickard, Samuel T. *Whittier-Land, A Handbook of North Essex.* Boston: Houghton Mifflin, 1904.

Stevens, James Stacy. *Whittier's Use of the Bible.* Orono, Maine: University of Maine Press, 1930. (The Maine Bulletin, Vol. XXXIII)

Williams, Cecil Brown. *Whittier's Use of Historical Material in Margaret Smith's Journal.* Chicago: University of Chicago Libraries, 1936.

ANALYSIS AND CRITICISM

Allen, Gay W. "John Greenleaf Whittier," *American Prosody.* New York: American Book Company, 1935.

Arms, George. "Whittier," *The Fields Were Green.* Stanford: Stanford University Press, 1953. [The most revealing and appreciative of all recent essays on Whittier.]

Clark, Harry Hayden (ed.). "Notes," *Major American Poets.* New York: American Book Co., 1936.

Jones, Howard Mumford. "Whittier Reconsidered," *Essex Institute Historical Collections* (October, 1957).

McEuen, Kathryn Anderson. "Whittier's Rhymes," *American Speech* (February, 1945).

Scott, Winfield Townley. "Poetry in American; a New Consideration of Whittier's Verse," *New England Quarterly* (June, 1934).

Waggoner, Hyatt H. "What I Had I Gave; Another Look at Whittier," *Essex Institute Historical Collections* (January, 1959).

Wells, Henry W. "Cambridge Culture and Folk Poetry," *The American Way of Poetry.* New York: Columbia University Press, 1943.

INDEX

Note: Historical and fictional characters from Whittier's works, other than those whose names appear in titles, are entered in small capital letters. Whittier's works are entered under his name.

139